Foreword by Bunny Grossinger

We Grossingers are known for our passion for food and, I'm afraid, for overconsumption too. Family memories of holidays at Grossinger's Hotel and Country Club in the Catskills belong to anyone who ever spent time there; they considered Grossinger's to be their home, too. As a bride in 1947 I had my first experience of dining with my new extended "family." Approximately 1,300 members, otherwise known as "guests," were now a permanent part of my new life.

In learning how to carve out a person_ celebrities, reporters, entertainers–I ha_ children with a semblance of the real wc_ would have lunch at the hotel at the "fa_ We would all show up to stand next to (the appropriate holiday greeting. Jennie national institution, famous for her "Hea_ television commercial for Grossinger rye

People would come to "the G" for every a resort, but the bottom line was the foc the dairy meal at Grossinger's or the se_ their own Grossinger family table. My share memories of Passovers when th_ staff went on strike and the fami_ chambermaids, but the Seder went off i

I have a passion for the preparation o_ reads recipes before I go to sleep. newspaper recipes. But that's as far as did–lots of tasting, feeling, and smellir synonymous in my psyche, you can ir publisher stepson, Richard Grossinger, this incredible book that you are abou

the healthy Jewish ookbook

_n the fragile remains of my last copy of my _he Art of Jewish Cooking. Jennie Grossinger wish cookbooks in the 1950s. Her book sold in aditional cookbook and it represented the era randparents. With the introduction of The _ok, a new classic opens a new era, the era of ldren, and even great-grandchildren. It is a _ provides a way to cook dishes that are good _ as well as the palate.

_ookbook is, at last, a cookbook for real people, _etails and family memories. With it, you can mptious meals, whether you observe kosher or exciting; the text clear, even mindful, of the _n on carbohydrates and glycemic indices. _es are doable. And, even if you never try out _kitchen, you can still devour the brilliant

_ok as pleasing as I do. I am confident that this _e hearts and minds of every Jewish soul-food _, Bon Appétit.

Michael van Straten

the
healthy Jewish
cookbook

100 delicious recipes from around the world

Recipes by Sally and Michael van Straten

Recipe photography by Jan Baldwin
Location photography by Vanessa Courtier

Frog, Ltd.
Berkeley, California

This book is dedicated to the memory of Kate, Ada, Sally, Gertie, Minnie, Leah, Harry, and Jimmy—the Greenberg brothers and sisters. They are all gone now, as is my father Louis whom they embraced into their family to make up for the loss of his own during the Holocaust of the Second World War. It's also in memory of their husbands and wives and two of my first cousins, Linda and Mark. We were a great and happy family for whom food was the cement that bound us all together, communal meals being the "band aid" that healed arguments and mended rifts. As long as there are children, grandchildren, and great-grandchildren who talk about their parents, aunts, and uncles and pass on the family recipes from generation to generation, they will always be with us.

First published in Great Britain 2005 by Kyle Cathie Limited, London

Frog, Ltd. books are distributed by North Atlantic Books, P.O. Box 12327, Berkeley, California 94712

Recipe photography © 2005 Jan Baldwin
Location photography © 2005 Vanessa Courtier
Photographs on pages 10, 13, 14 © The Jewish Museum, London
Photographs on pages 1, 18-19, 44-45, 68-69, 92-93, 124-125, 142-143, 160 © 2005 Vanessa Courtier, objects courtesy of The Jewish Museum, London
Photograph on page 34 © 2003 Steve Lee
Book design © 2005 Kyle Cathie Limited

Senior editor Muna Reyal
Art direction and design Vanessa Courtier
Recipe photography Jan Baldwin
Location and chapter opener photography Vanessa Courtier
Home economist David Morgan
Styling Róisín Nield
Copyeditor Jamie Ambrose
Editorial assistant Jennifer Wheatley
Production Sha Huxtable and Alice Holloway

Color reproduction by Chromagraphic
Printed and bound in China by C & C Offset Printing Company Ltd.

Distributed to the book trade by Publishers Group West

Library of Congress Cataloging-in-Publication Data
Van Straten, Michael.
  The healthy Jewish cookbook : 100 delicious recipes from around the world / by Michael van Straten ; foreword by Bunny Grossinger.
    p. cm.
  Summary: "A modern look at Jewish cooking, featuring a nutritious, low-fat approach to cooking traditional Jewish dishes from around the world"--Provided by publisher.
  Includes index.
  ISBN 1-58394-150-9 (pbk.)
  1. Cookery, Jewish. 2. Low-fat diet--Recipes. I. Title.
  TX724.V36 2006
  641.5'676--dc22
                                                            2005027237

10 9 8 7 6 5 4 3 2 1

contents

My mother's healthy kitchen

My mother, Kate, was a wonderful cook—mostly. True, she could boil the life out of any vegetable and happily incinerate any piece of grilled meat and turn pasta into a glutinous mass. But when it came to soups, stews, casseroles, cakes, cookies or puddings, she was infallible. When she made strudel you could almost see through the paper-thin sheets of dough. She never trusted any butcher enough to buy ground meat and I still remember happy days turning the handle on the old Spong meat grinder with its interchangeable blades and the mark it always left when it was clamped to the kitchen tabletop, in spite of the folded-up newspaper.

Kate was one of six sisters and two brothers who grew up in the tenement buildings of London's East End when it was the center of Jewish life. Brothers Harry and Jimmy and four of the sisters, Kate, Ada, Sally, and Gertie, were married. The other two, Minnie and Leah, remained single. My aunt Leah was the cleverest one by far, well-read and intellectual, but she was the one who stayed behind to care for my elderly grandparents and then became the universal aunt, traveling from sister to sister whenever help was needed or illness struck. She spent many years living with us and as a small boy I think I was often awful to her but came to love and respect her dearly as I grew a bit more sensible.

All the sisters were great cooks, each with their own specialties, and of course, as happens in all Jewish families, the husbands of the sisters and all their relatives, and the wives of the brothers with all theirs too, together with all their various offspring, became one huge family of *mespucha*—an untranslatable Yiddish word which embraces any relative of any relative and all their relatives under the one extended family umbrella. Gatherings of the *mespucha*, whether for birthdays, anniversaries, bar mitzvahs, weddings or funerals, were exciting, noisy, and wonderful events with simultaneous conversations in Yiddish, Dutch, and English with a host of European accents.

My mother's family was never orthodox and worshipped at the Reform Synagogue in the Oxford and St. George's Club run by Sir Basil and Lady Henriques. This was a center for religious, social, and sporting activities for the whole of the poor Jewish community in the East End and our family was heavily involved in many aspects of this wonderful institution. Early in the war my parents and I moved out of London to the rural tranquillity of Tring in Hertfordshire. We didn't keep separate pans, dishes, cutlery, and crockery for milk and meat, but my mother never served milk and meat together and no forbidden food ever entered her kitchen. Kosher meat and poultry came from London by train, or was brought by my father when he came back from work on Fridays, together with a selection of cousins who wanted a weekend in the country.

Opposite: *Kate and Louis van Straten, photographed by Boris, September 13, 1937.*
My mother made her wedding dress and the collar, sleeves, and hem were beaded with rows of tiny seed pearls—every one sewn on by hand.
Below: *Me aged five with my mother and father. My mouth is firmly shut to hide missing front teeth, lost when I fell out of a taxi outside the John Barnes store in Finchley Road, now Waitrose.*

There was a number of Jewish families in Tring during the war, enough to run a small synagogue in a wonderful building that used to be the Gaiety Theatre and there was nearly always the required ten men (a *minyon*) to hold a formal service. After the war most returned to London, but my parents stayed for another 20 years. I was lucky enough to be educated at one of the oldest public schools in England in the nearby town of Berkhamsted. Unlike the author Graham Greene, who hated the school and whose father had been headmaster, I loved it and spent an extremely happy ten years there. In a total of 600 or more boys, only six of us were Jews—they still had quotas in those days—but in spite of a bit of juvenile anti-Semitism, especially from the Irish Catholic lads, there was no discrimination within the school. A rabbi came every Sunday morning to hold religious classes, which included two or three girls from our sister school, and that was our only alternative to attending the school chapel service.

Although no kosher food was available, my wonderful housemaster, the late Monty Fry, understood the problems and whenever ham, pork, bacon, or other forbidden foods were on the menu, there was always an alternative for me and the two other Jewish boys in the boarding house. The real fun started when I took hordes of my contemporaries home to mother. These were youngsters of every race, creed, and color whose far-flung homes in India, Africa, Asia, and South America made family visits impossible for them. My mother adopted them all and whether I turned up with one or four extra mouths, she fed them. I meet old school friends today who, 50 years on, talk about my mother's wonderful cooking and how much at home they felt in the very Jewish atmosphere of our house.

As the only Jewish boy growing up in a very conservative small country town, life wasn't always easy and it was sometimes embarrassing to ask a friend's mother what was in the sandwiches, or what meat was in the stew, but they were all very understanding and soon learned that there were foods that I didn't eat. One terrible exception was being invited to join a girlfriend with her family at a very posh lunch in an expensive local restaurant. Her father was a large choleric man whose equally large moustache testified to his RAF service in the war, and was given to drinking Black Velvet—half Guinness, half champagne—out of a 20 ounce silver mug early in the morning. I coped with the hors d'oeuvre as I managed to hide the shrimp under the shredded lettuce and squash it all down so it looked as if I'd eaten them, but to my horror the main course was specially ordered Lobster Thermidore, which I had to turn down. The father ranted and raved and shouted so much that I left the room scarlet with embarrassment and didn't see his beautiful daughter, whom I thought was the love of my life, for another 40 years.

I can't claim to have led a blameless life of kosher eating, but to this day I've never eaten shellfish or pork and can't imagine ever doing so.

Thanks to General Franco   If it weren't for the fascist dictator General Franco, I wouldn't be here. In the late 1930s my mother, her partner in their wedding-dress business, and their best friend planned a holiday in Spain.

With bags packed and tickets booked, the best friend was refused a visa at the very last moment as she was born in Russia and had a Russian passport. The three smart young girls decided to go to Holland and in the seaside town of Scheveningen, my mother met my father on the beach where he was a performing gymnast. In spite of not speaking a word of each other's language, they fell in love, my father followed her back to England, and it wasn't long before they were married. I arrived in 1939.

I never knew my father's parents nor any of his enormous family, except for his youngest brother Jo. Though I owed my existence to one fascist, another took the lives of 150 members of my father's family—parents, grandparents, brothers, sisters, nieces, nephews, uncles, aunts, and every other relative. My uncle Jo and his wife Henny were hidden by the most extraordinarily brave Catholic family in the cellars of their house, where they lived on potato peel, tulip bulbs, and dead rats for two years.

I think for all Jews the taste, smell, and sight of traditional foods are a window onto the very soul of Jewishness. Happily my mother spent enough time with her mother-in-law before the war to learn many of the skills of Dutch Jewish cooking, with its Asian and Iberian influences. For my father, these "tastes of home" were the links with his childhood and lost family. Food memories play a powerful role in the Jewish psyche, serving as reminders of past times, good and bad, of communities destroyed and families lost. When I cook one of my aunt Henny's recipes, the smells transport me to her tiny kitchen in Rotterdam; I can see the view across the lake from her window; I imagine sitting with my uncle Jo as a seven-year-old while he taught me to play chess; I relive the moment of stepping out of Rotterdam station in 1947 and seeing hardly a single building standing; I still feel the thrill of ice skating with the next-door neighbor's son along the canals to his school.

Thanks, I'm sure, to my mother's wonderful cooking and the huge love of her entire family, my father was an amazingly fit, strong, and healthy man till he died at the age of 87. He never spoke to me about the loss of his family or the guilt he must have felt at having escaped the horrors of the Holocaust. To my great joy, my father formed a very close bond with my second wife, Sally, a rather lapsed Irish Catholic. One evening they had a meal together and for no obvious reason he started to talk about his family, the war, and his terrible sense of loss. Once he started there was no stopping and Sally said she hardly spoke a word for four hours. Father had received some letters written on the transport trains and from the death camps. He also spoke to some survivors about those terrible times, but I don't think he ever really came to terms with losing his family and every one of his contemporary school friends. Apart from his one surviving brother there was no one to whom he could say about his early years, "Do you remember when…"

To this day Sally finds it hard to understand how Louis, my dad, could ever laugh or smile again after all that tragedy.

Above: *Dutch treat—my lovely mother Kate (left) with her business partner Elsie and best friend Leah (right). This was taken on a girls' holiday in Holland in the summer of 1936. Just a few days later Kate met my father, they fell desperately in love, and he followed her back to England.*

Going back to its roots

To Jews and non-Jews alike, the idea of a healthy Jewish cookbook must seem like the impossible dream. But how wrong can they be? The belief that all Jewish food is "a heart attack on a plate" stems from limited encounters with the Jewish food of northern and Eastern Europe. Heavy, fatty, salty, or overly-sweet dishes filled with chicken fat, corned beef, cream cheese, pickled herrings, and strudel were the products only of 20th-century Europe.

The health hazards came with affluence. Having heating fuel and living in northern Europe, the UK, and America reduced the enormous need for calories that were essential to survive the bitter winters of Eastern Europe. Having money meant adding more meat and fewer vegetables, beans, and grains to the stew or casserole. Gradually the physical demands of work declined so that today there is no longer a calorie requirement listed for "heavy manual labor." Machines have taken over and they need the calories, not the operators.

Baker's treat: Bagels and all sorts of other Jewish specialties were the foundation of Henry Goldring's shop in Upper Clapton Road, north London, when it opened just around the turn of the 20th century.

In earlier times, food was scarce and rationed by lack of money and availability. Just as with the British during the Second World War, food rationing meant a healthier diet. Even the dreaded *cholent*, with its artery-clogging saturated fat and heart-stoppingly massive portions served by mothers-in-law, started life as the healthiest of dishes. It originated in medieval France and, according to the great and academic food writer Claudia Roden, the name is derived from the French *chaud* and *lent*, which mean hot and slow respectively. It was taken to the village bakery on Friday afternoon and left to cook overnight, ready to collect at the end of the Sabbath day. This was a dish of beans, lentils, and root vegetables, and in the good times may have had a scrap of meat for flavor. But it was virtually fat-free.

In spite of this, the all-too-common perception of Jewish cooking has spread through the highly influential German-Jewish community of the early 20th century and the enormous influx of Jewish refugees fleeing the pogroms of Eastern Europe and Russia from the mid 19th century onwards. But this ignores the Sephardi Jews, whose cultural and culinary contributions to Jewish eating have historically been underrated. In truth these are the Jews often overlooked by their Ashkenazi brethren. The Sephardim were Jews who settled in the Spanish peninsula, the Ottoman Empire—mainly Greece and Turkey—the north African countries of Morocco, Tunisia, Libya, and Algeria, and finally there were those who went to Persia and Babylon. Fed by the Diaspora, these communities flourished and, while keeping to the Jewish dietary laws, they adopted the local foods and culinary traditions. The desert and its meager produce defined the food of the Yemenite Jews, whereas in Mesopotamia, the heart of the fertile crescent which saw man's first successful agriculture, there were lush pastures, rich crops, and abundant fish. Sephardi settlers around the Mediterranean adapted their cuisine to the Mediterranean climate and have produced some of the healthiest Jewish food of all. Jews traveled the silk routes and settled in China, and communities grew up in India, and in Persia, Egypt, east Africa, and the Far East. Jewish cuisine spread and prospered but remained virtually unknown to the world of Ashkenazi Jewry.

The Ashkenazi Jews were those who moved further to the north and east, choosing to live in Germany, France, Italy, and the United Kingdom. As the ravages of the Crusades forced them eastwards to escape slaughter and persecution, they ended up in Poland and Russia where, because of the extremely harsh climate, their food was very different. Not for them delicate spices, fruits, and salads, but rib-sticking dishes of sauerkraut, root vegetables, dumplings, smoked and salted meat and fish.

Bagels, lox (smoked salmon) and cream cheese—real fusion food

As much as the innovative Australian chefs like to take the credit for the cooking cult of fusion food, I'm afraid they're wrong. Imaginative, inventive, and wonderful though it is, their melding together of flavors from the Pacific Rim, Europe, and Australia was pre-dated by several thousand years when the Red Sea parted and the Diaspora of Jews began. The strict requirements of Jewish dietary laws determined how Jews ate wherever they settled in the world and this resulted in the fusion of foods from many lands.

When the Jews traveled they took many of their creative culinary practices with them, so the hot spicy dishes from the kosher kitchens of Cochin, India migrated to east Africa, whereas most South African Jews came from northern Europe, especially from Holland. This is where the fascinating pieces of the jigsaw start fitting together. Consider that the Cochin Jews were heavily involved in the spice trade, dealing especially in turmeric, cloves, nutmeg, cinnamon, and pepper, and during the late 17th and most of the 18th centuries they worked with the highly successful Dutch East India Company. These exotic cargoes were stored in magnificent buildings lining the great canals of Amsterdam, then the center of the European spice trade. Some of the Indian Jews ended up in Holland, but many other Dutch Jews originally came from Spain and Portugal, where the powerful effect of the Moorish occupation influenced the herbs and spices used in cooking. Still more Jews came to Holland from Eastern Europe, bringing with them their tastes for sausage, sauerkraut, and hearty winter dishes essential in such a bitter climate. They were using garlic, onion, caraway, dill, fennel, parsley, and all the other north European culinary herbs.

Put all this into the same stockpot and you have the ultimate fusion cooking which became so popular that many dishes found their way into non-Jewish Dutch kitchens. When the Boers—Dutch farmers who were mostly non-conformist Christians—went to South Africa, together with both Ashkenazi and Sephardi Jews, they took with them a Europeanized form of Dutch-Indian-Moorish cooking which is commonplace throughout South Africa.

Purely by coincidence, I spent a number of years working in a therapy center that occupied a wonderful 17th-century spice warehouse in Amsterdam. Though the building had not been used for its original purpose for more than 100 years, the magical aroma of spices had seeped into its very fabric. Often I was the only person there overnight, and in the small, still hours, when the building creaked and groaned on its 300-year-old wooden piles deep beneath the water, I could still smell the spices and imagine enormous heaps of burlap sacks bulging with their exotic cargo.

The popular image of the "wandering Jew" is not far from the truth as it seems that almost every Jew has inherited the traveling gene and they move with equal ease from village to village or from town to town as they do from country to country or continent to continent. Whether forced by persecution and pogroms, or undertaken for purposes of trade and business or simply to satisfy a wanderlust, Jews have traveled to the four corners of the earth in the past 3,000 years. Wherever they end up, they take with them the religious demands of the kosher kitchen and the culinary traditions of the place they leave and merge these two, seamlessly, with the food available in their new homes.

Nowhere is this more obvious than in New York, the original mecca of American Jewry. In the early 1900s, European Jews flooded into America, mostly arriving in New York with little more than the clothes they stood in. It was here that Ashkenazi Jewish cooking had the most profound effect on the eating habits of the American nation. Husbands, brothers, cousins, fathers, and even grandfathers were the first to arrive and it was their task to find work and homes so their families could follow. To serve the huge appetites of these hardworking single men, the New York deli was born. These Jewish-run kosher eateries gave these men their tastes of home: barley soup you could stand a spoon in; corned beef and pastrami in fist-thick sandwiches; stuffed cabbage; sauerkraut; *gefilte* fish—boiled or fried fishcakes; salamis and sausages of every shape; chopped liver; pickled herrings and smoked salmon, all served with mountains of rye bread and dill pickles. As the Jews spread across America, they took their delis with them and they soon became the place to eat for every immigrant group that followed.

These are the roots of fusion cooking.

Healthy kosher food

I've tried to find the healthiest of kosher Jewish recipes to include in this book, but I've also endeavored to make sure that they're simple and delicious. This I hope will encourage Jews to eat more healthily and non-Jews to enjoy these fascinating foods, some of which date back to almost a thousand years before the Christian era, and which combine the traditions of Jewish cooking with flavors from the entire world. That said, the basic principles of kosher cooking are healthy, particularly those which forbid the consumption of milk and meat foods in the same meal. This simple practice immediately reduces the amount of saturated and artery-clogging fat consumed. If you want to finish your dinner with cheese, you must eat low-fat fish rather than meat. If you want cream on your fruit salad, tart, or pudding, then you may not eat sausage, hamburger, salami, or any other form of meat beforehand.

From the biblical lands flowing with milk and honey, Jewish cooks have had a love affair with good food. Every fruit and vegetable, nuts, seeds, and all sorts of grains, herbs, and spices feature in the repertoire of Jewish cooking. Sea and fresh-water fish, olive oil, scrupulous attention to hygiene, the religious requirements of the dietary laws, and the mandatory, frequent washing of hands all contribute to the healthiness of the best of Jewish cooking.

Dried fruits have always been a favorite and these are highly concentrated sources of powerfully protective nutrients. The foods which are your best defense against heart disease, high blood pressure, strokes, many forms of cancer, arthritis, and aging are those with the highest ORAC scores. ORAC (Oxygen Radical Absorbance Capacity) is a way of measuring the protective value of whole foods devised by scientists at Tufts University Research Center on Aging in Boston, Massachusetts. Best are the dark-colored fruits and vegetables. The average British diet provides about 1,500 ORAC units a day, but optimum protection comes from 5,000 units. Blueberries, strawberries, spinach, Brussels sprouts, plums, dried apricots, raisins, and garlic are abundant in these plant chemicals, but richest of all are prunes. Throughout the book you'll find useful information in the introductions to the recipes.

For the ultra-orthodox Jew, there is no compromise over the laws of Kashrut and anyone that observant will not need detailed explanations of the dietary laws. But just to paint a broad picture of what is involved in kosher eating, here are some of the basic facts. The basic laws of Kashrut were handed down by God to the Jews, sanctified in the holy scroll of the Torah, and amplified by generations of rabbis throughout the centuries. These laws are accepted without question and although it's possible to find reasons of health and hygiene within the biblical commandments, rabbis tell us that it's pointless to search for deeper meanings. The laws of Kashrut are God's words and need no questioning.

Fishy story: In London's East End, fish was a staple diet food for much of the Jewish population. Obviously not kosher—orthodox Jews don't eat oysters—Henry Phillips, seen here with three of his children, was a popular member of the local community. This picture was taken in 1950.

Meat The only meat allowed comes from animals with cloven feet that chew the cud. So ox, cow, veal, mutton, lamb, goat, and the more exotic gazelle, antelope, and mountain sheep are all allowed, as, theoretically is venison. These animals must be slaughtered in the ritual manner by having their throats cut and this must be done under the supervision of an approved *shochet* (slaughterer). It's widely believed that the hindquarters cannot be eaten, which is why it's seldom possible to eat a good kosher steak. But they can be eaten provided they're properly prepared by having the sciatic nerve removed, in which case they would be permissible.

In the Jewish religion the most potent symbol of life is blood, and its consumption is absolutely forbidden, which is why all blood must be drained immediately at the time of slaughter. The meat then has to be soaked and salted or, in the case of variety meats like liver, broiled under a very high heat so that no blood remains.

Poultry Chicken, duck, turkey, and goose are permitted, but all birds of prey and scavengers are not. Game birds that have been hunted or wild fowl are not kosher unless they've been bred and slaughtered in the ritual manner.

Fish Kosher fish must have removable scales and fins, so all shellfish and crustaceans, along with octopus, squid, eel, monkfish (angler fish), ray, rock salmon, skate, sturgeon, swordfish, and turbot are among those not regarded as being kosher.

Deli desire: Salt beef, gefilte fish, chopped liver, egg and onions and a variety of sandwiches were on sale at Abrahamson's restaurant in London's theatreland. This photograph was taken in the early 1930s.

Dairy products These may not be consumed at the same time as meat, though the length of time you should wait does vary from one community to another. You can't cook meat and milk together, and the period after meat before you can consume milk ranges from two to six hours. You can eat a dairy meal and then a meat meal without a waiting period, but a milk-based appetizer and a meat main course would not be acceptable. There are non-dairy substitutes like kosher margarine, non-dairy creamers, and milk substitutes, but they are generally high in saturated fats, extremely unhealthy, and I don't ever use them. Soy products are a great alternative and certified kosher versions are more widely available now. For the strictly orthodox, it's necessary to use kosher cheese, which is made without animal rennet, and it's also important to avoid dairy products like yogurts which may contain animal-based gelatin.

Pareve foods These are foods that are neither meat nor dairy and can be eaten with any type of meal. They include all fruits and vegetables, grains, eggs, and fish (see above), but of course if you cook them with butter or animal fat, or serve them with a cream sauce, they then become milk or meat foods.

The religious festivals

There are many Jewish festivals that have their own food rituals. To the orthodox Jew, they all have immense importance, but to all Jews, even the least observant, there are some that never lose their significance. The enduring qualities of *Shabbat*—the ushering-in of Sabbath on Friday night—are the cornerstone of Judaism, bringing light, blessings, and peace. As one of the Ten Commandments, observing the Sabbath is the Jew's acknowledgement that God created the world in six days and rested on the seventh. Lighting the candles, blessing the bread and wine, and sitting down with the family on Friday night is an instantly recognizable ceremony wherever Jews are found, even in the farthest outposts of human occupation.

No matter how simple, humble, rich, or poor the table may be, it is the custom to cover it with a white cloth. Add the Sabbath candlesticks and the altar-like symbolism is immediately apparent. These rituals all help to reinforce the religious aspects of these ceremonial meals. The mother's traditional blessing of the Sabbath candles and the presence of the entire family around the "altar" are the catalyst which hardens the cement binding families and communities together. The universality of the language of Jewish prayer makes a stranger feel at home at a Sabbath table or a synagogue anywhere in the world. I've always felt that the Catholic church made a great mistake when they abandoned the Latin mass, which made it accessible to worshippers in every country.

There are many festivals throughout the year. Here are details of just a few of the most important. New Year and Yom Kippur (the Day of Atonement) have deep meanings for even the least-observant Jews. Those who hardly ever set foot inside a synagogue will do so on one of those days.

Rosh Hashanah—New Year   This occurs on the first and second days of the Hebrew month *Tishrei*, which is normally in September or October. At this time, Jews throughout the world pray for a new year of health, peace, and prosperity. It's a time of judgment and a time when we seek God's guidance to help us live better lives in the year to come.

This is also the time when the *Shofar* (ram's horn) is blown in the synagogue—a hundred blasts during the two days of services. This is the most ancient of all wind instruments and its plaintive sound is highly symbolic. During this festival it's traditional to eat sweet foods as an indication of sweet things to come in the New Year. *Challah* (braided bread covered in poppy seeds) dipped in honey, slices of apple coated with honey, sweet fresh fruits, and *tzimmes* (carrots cooked with honey and orange juice) are all eaten. The meal is often finished with a pomegranate in the hope that our good deeds may increase like the seeds of this delicious fruit. Honey cake is another traditional New Year treat.

Yom Kippur   This is the most solemn day in the Jewish calendar, ten days after New Year. It begins just before sunset and, until sunset the next day, it's forbidden to eat or drink. The orthodox also abstain from sex, from using perfumes, and from wearing leather shoes. This is a time of confession, memorial prayers for the dead, and judgment for the coming year. At the end of the fast, the whole family gathers for a meal of true celebration.

Sukkot   Taking place on the 15th and 16th of the Hebrew month *Tishrei*, this is the Jewish equivalent of harvest festival. Traditionally, Jews build a covered shelter outside where for a week all meals are eaten. The roof should be made of evergreen branches like laurel, ivy, leylandii or any other suitable plant material, and the walls could be plywood, plastic sheeting, canvas, or any other temporary material, though some part of the roof must be open to the sky. The building of this *sukkah* is very much a part of the festival.

Hanukkah   This begins on the 25th day of the Hebrew month *Kislev*, corresponding to November/December, and frequently coincides with Christmas.

The great symbol of Hanukkah is the *menorah*, a candlestick with eight branches and a separate holder for the candle used to light the others. Here we celebrate the victory of a tiny band of Maccabees against the entire Greek army. After defeating the Greeks they set about restoring the defiled holy temple but they could find only one tiny jar of oil that hadn't been defiled by the invading soldiers and it was enough to light the *menorah* for just one day. But a miracle occurred and the oil burned for eight whole days, after which freshly pressed oil was prepared. This miracle celebrates the defeat of the Greeks who were desperate to discredit the Jewish deity and convert all to the worship of their gods. Each night a candle is lit and by the eighth night, all eight illuminate the home.

Because of the oil, this is when fried foods are popular—potato *latkes* (pancakes), small fried doughnuts, and cheese *latkes* are common foods. This is also a time when children get presents including money, some of which they are expected to give to charity.

Pesach   Passover is celebrated from the 15th to the 22nd of the Hebrew month *Nissan*, corresponding to March/April, and often coincides with Easter. This is the great celebration of the exodus from ancient Egypt and the giving of the law on Mount Sinai. As the Jews left Egypt, the Egyptians were afflicted by the plagues, the sea opened to let the Jews pass, then closed over the pursuing Egyptian horsemen. Passover celebrates this deliverance from bondage and the most important religious service takes place in the home. This is the time when no leavened bread but only *matzo* is eaten. These flat crisp sheets of baked dough are a reminder that when the Jews fled Egypt, there was no time to let the bread rise, so it was made without yeast and baked like crackers. The *Seder* service, as it is known, takes place with family, friends, and neighbors seated around the diningroom table on the first two evenings of Passover. The story of the exodus is retold, mainly for the benefit of the children so that each generation can pass it on to the next.

Six special foods are eaten, normally arranged on a plate designed to hold them. These are roasted chicken neck or lamb shank representing the Paschal lamb eaten on the eve of the exodus; a hard-boiled egg for the offering in the holy temple; bitter herbs (usually fresh horseradish, Belgian endive or bitter greens), lest we forget the bitterness and slavery of our ancestors in Egypt; *charoset*, chopped apples, nuts, and red wine mixed to remind us how the Jews labored under the Pharaoh to make bricks without straw; a non-bitter vegetable like raw onion or potato; and finally, extra bitter herbs are made into a sandwich with *matzo*.

Although not a religious requirement, it's common for hard-boiled eggs to be served in salt water as a reminder of the tears shed for the suffering of the Jews in bondage and of the Egyptians who perished in the plagues and the sea.

The meal itself is eaten interspersed with various readings and songs from the Passover book, the *Haggadah*.

This service is of great importance in the religious upbringing of all Jewish children, but as families become more dispersed and communities less cohesive, there are now many communal *Seder* services conducted under the auspices of synagogues and a variety of Jewish organizations. Any Jew who hasn't sat through a *Seder* for years, or any non-Jew who has never been to one but has a Jewish friend, should try to participate in this, one of the most uplifting and meaningful of religious celebrations.

Salt and pepper pots These earthenware containers were made in Leeds around 1820. Meals are a very important part of Judaism and are treated almost as a religious occasion. The table symbolizes the altar at the temple for the show bread. The inscription on the pot on the far left says, "This is the table which is before the Lord" while the inscription on the other pot is from Numbers and Deuteronomy and is a quote from the *Shema*, the most important of the Jewish prayers, "And you shall eat and you shall bless the Lord your God."

appetizers

Radishes and quail eggs

Serves 4

24 quail eggs
24 smallish radishes, trimmed
1/3 cup (3/4 stick) unsalted butter,
*   softened*
1 teaspoon celery salt
*   or 2 tablespoons celery seeds,*
*   crushed*

Although quail are biblical birds, they were almost certainly never bred in the Middle East, but were trapped in their exhausted state after migrating across the Mediterranean. These small birds, related to the pheasant, were native to parts of Europe and China. Their culinary history goes back to ancient Rome. Quail were, and still are, popular in France for their eggs as well as their meat.

In this recipe, the eggs are combined with radishes in the traditional French way of eating radishes with butter and salt.

Method Put the eggs into cold water, bring quickly to a boil, and simmer for 4 minutes. Plunge immediately into cold water and let cool for about 3 minutes. Peel carefully.

Arrange the eggs and radishes alternately on a serving dish. If using butter and celery salt, mix the salt into the butter.

Serve the eggs and radishes in the middle of the table with the celery butter in a separate dish. If using butter and celery seeds, serve in separate bowls for dipping.

Health note Radishes stimulate liver function, and each quail egg provides 158 calories, plus protein and lots of iron and vitamin A as well as B vitamins.

Egg and onion with cilantro

Serves 3-4

4 hard-boiled eggs, well mashed
6 medium scallions, trimmed
*   and finely chopped*
2 tablespoons extra-virgin olive oil
Black pepper
1 tablespoon finely chopped
*   cilantro*

Here's another very traditional Jewish appetizer that is equally at home at a bar mitzvah, wedding, or funeral. I'm sure previous generations weren't aware of the benefits of combining egg with onion, but in fact all members of the allium genus (onions, garlic, shallots, scallions, leeks, and chives) contain natural chemicals that help the body's elimination of cholesterol.

This dish is normally made with parsley, but an Indian Jewish friend always uses coriander leaves (cilantro) in her recipe and it gives an unexpected peppery bite.

Method Mix together the eggs and onions. Drizzle in the olive oil and mix well. Season with pepper to taste. Serve sprinkled with the chopped cilantro.

Chickpeas on spinach

Serves 2-3

2 ¼ pounds baby spinach

2 tablespoons unsalted butter

1 ⅓ cups canned chickpeas
  (drained weight)

1 large sprig of sage

4 tablespoons extra-virgin olive oil

Black pepper

Throughout the Middle East, chickpeas are a staple food, as they are in India, Latin America, Spain, and Italy. Like all the legumes, they're inexpensive, highly nutritious, and amazing value for the money. They're low in calories, virtually fat-free, and an excellent source of fiber, especially the soluble fiber which is so important in controlling cholesterol levels.

Method Wash the spinach (even if it's "ready-washed"). Melt the butter in a large pot. Add the spinach with just the water clinging to its leaves. Cover and heat gently, shaking the pot occasionally, until the spinach wilts–about 5 minutes.

Meanwhile, drain the chickpeas and rinse thoroughly. Put into a separate pan with the sage, add just enough water to cover, and heat through gently for about 5-6 minutes.

Drain the spinach well, arrange on serving plates, and drizzle half the olive oil over it.

Drain the chickpeas, removing the sage, and divide between the serving plates on top of the spinach.

Drizzle over them the remaining oil and season with black pepper to taste.

Health note Chickpeas contain lots of folic acid, protein, and complex carbohydrates, so they have a low glycemic index, which means they provide slow-release energy and cause a minimal increase in blood-sugar levels and insulin production. For this reason, they help protect against type-2 diabetes. Chickpeas also contain a group of chemicals called isoflavones: estrogen-like compounds that reduce the risk of osteoporosis and other symptoms of menopause.

Avocado-stuffed tomatoes

Serves 4

*4 beefsteak tomatoes (or 8 smaller
  ones)*

2 medium avocados

4 scallions, finely sliced

1 small garlic clove, finely chopped

Juice of 1 small lemon

Pinch of paprika

2 dashes of Tabasco sauce

For modern Jews, the popularity of the avocado is the result of the massive cultivation of this amazing fruit in Israel and California. It's most unfortunate that so many people think of the avocado as a high-fat, high-calorie, and unhealthy food, when the exact opposite is true. This luscious, creamy fruit is probably the healthiest of all; ounce for ounce, it's the most nutritious of all the most popular fruits. There's also hardly any sodium in this recipe and it's wonderful food for children of all ages.

Method Slice the tops off the tomatoes, scoop out the insides, and discard the tough membranes but reserve the pulp. Dry the cut tomatoes gently with paper towels.

Cut the avocados in half and scrape the flesh into a bowl. Add the tomato pulp and the remaining ingredients and mash well.

Spoon into the open tomatoes.

Health note Avocados provide 60 percent more potassium than bananas, lots of magnesium (for energy), folic acid, fiber, riboflavin, and vitamins B6, C, and E. Most of the fat is monounsaturated, which lowers the dangerous LDL cholesterol and raises the heart-protective HDL cholesterol. Avocado is also one of the richest sources of beta-sitosterol, which helps lower blood pressure.

Peanuts with green beans

Serves 4

3 tablespoons olive oil

1 onion, finely chopped

1 large garlic clove, very finely chopped

³/4 cup unsalted, shelled peanuts

18 ounces green beans, trimmed and cut into 1-inch lengths (about 3 ¹/2 cups)

1 small green pepper, chopped

Salt and black pepper

1 tablespoon each finely chopped flat-leaf parsley and cilantro

This is a typical recipe from the remarkable black Jews of Ethiopia. They lived in virtual isolation until the Israelis brought them back to Israel in an amazing rescue operation which began with 12,000 in 1984 and culminated in 1991, when the remaining 14,000 were repatriated by the Israeli government. Known as Falashas—now considered a derogatory term by Ethiopian Jews—they believe they're descendants of Menelik, the son of King Solomon and the Queen of Sheba. This recipe is an example of reverse migration, as the Ethiopians brought their ancient traditions back to the land of their forefathers.

Method Heat the oil in a heavy frying pan and sauté the onion, garlic, and nuts gently until the onions are soft. Add the beans and green pepper and continue to cook, stirring continuously, until the beans are tender, adding a little more olive oil if necessary. Season to taste.

Serve with the herbs scattered on top.

Health note Contrary to popular perception, peanuts are extremely healthy, as they provide slow-release energy, protect against diabetes, and help with any weight-loss regime.

Brazilian bean salad

Serves 4-6

14 ounces (about 2 1/2 cups)
quinoa, well rinsed and drained

18 ounces French green beans,
topped and tailed (about
3 1/2–4 cups)

Salt

1 tablespoon pumpkin seeds

1 tablespoon sesame seeds

3 tablespoons extra-virgin olive oil

Juice of 1 lemon

Before traveling up the Amazon to study the medicinal herbs of the rain forest Indians, I spent a few days in Rio where I went to a jewelery store to buy my wife a present. The owner turned out to be Jewish and invited me to join his family for the Sabbath meal on Friday evening. That was my first introduction to quinoa. Like buckwheat, this isn't a grain but the seed from a very distant relative of spinach. Cultivated for more than 5,000 years in South America, it was the staple food of the Incas. Although it's a fairly recent arrival in Europe and America, you'll find it in health food stores and many supermarkets.

Method Toast the quinoa in a dry frying pan, stirring continuously for 3-4 minutes. Put it into a large saucepan, cover with 3 cups cold water, bring to a boil, cover, and simmer until translucent, when the germ spirals out of each grain (about 15 minutes), adding extra boiling water if necessary. Drain if necessary and let cool.

Boil the beans in lightly salted water until *al dente*–about 2 minutes. Refresh in cold water and drain. Mix together the quinoa and beans and sprinkle with the pumpkin and sesame seeds. Drizzle with the olive oil. Pour the lemon juice over it to taste.

Health note Quinoa is extremely rich in iron and potassium, and also contains B vitamins, zinc, and magnesium. Unlike most grains, it provides almost complete protein (as well as being delicious to eat).

Falafel

Serves 4

3/4 cup dried chickpeas

3/4 cup canned chickpeas

1 teaspoon paprika

1 teaspoon celery seeds, crushed

1 tablespoon finely chopped
   fresh cilantro

1 tablespoon finely chopped
   flat-leaf parsley

1 garlic clove, crushed

1 medium onion, chopped

About 1/2 cup canola (rapeseed)
   or olive oil

1 iceberg lettuce, finely shredded
   or romaine lettuce leaves

4 plum tomatoes, chopped,
   for garnishing

Lemon slices, for garnishing

This ancient dish has its origins shrouded in antiquity. In many parts of the Middle East, it was traditionally made from dried fava beans, which are a staple of Lebanese cuisine. It was probably the Yemenite Jews who first introduced falafel to Israel, although it was, in fact, one of the most popular foods of the Palestinians. So quickly did these delicious nuggets of chickpeas, herbs, and spices endear themselves to the Israelis that as early as the celebrations of their first independence day, May 14, 1947, there were falafel sellers in Zion Square providing food for the gathered crowds.

For the orthodox Jew, falafel is one of the useful *pareve* foods—meaning they can be eaten with either milk or meat meals. This homemade delicacy is entirely different from those heavy, dense and often greasy commercial products. It is definitely worth the time and effort.

Method Soak the chickpeas in water for at least 8 hours. Drain and whizz them in a food-processor along with the canned chickpeas, spices, herbs, garlic, and onion. Don't overblend, otherwise you'll end up with a purée that makes a very dense falafel. Taking a tablespoon at a time, make the mixture into balls about the size of a walnut.

Heat the oil in a wok or deep frying pan and fry the falafels in batches until golden—about 5 minutes per batch. Drain each batch on paper towels and keep warm until all the mixture is used.

Serve on a bed of shredded lettuce, topped with chopped tomatoes and garnished with lemon slices.

Spiced eggplant purée

Serves 4

*2 medium eggplants, peeled
    and cubed*
Salt and black pepper
1 1/2-inch piece of ginger root
1 small red or green chile
About 3 tablespoons olive oil
1 large onion, finely chopped
2 garlic cloves, finely chopped
1 teaspoon ground turmeric
1/2 teaspoon ground coriander
1/2 teaspoon ground cumin
1 tablespoon garam masala
*2 tomatoes, peeled, seeded,
    and crushed*
Nan and/or chapati, for serving

This wonderful purée is a typical food of the Jewish people who came from Iraq during the 17th century. They settled in Calcutta, where they prospered and, typical of Jews all over the world, soon fused their culinary skills with the traditions of their adopted homeland. Sadly, their community is now quite small, but the traditional bread made by Jewish bakers is still produced today in non-Jewish bakeries—but not on Saturdays. You can follow their traditions and eat this purée with Indian breads such as nan and chapati.

Method Put the eggplants in a colander, sprinkling the layers with salt to encourage the expulsion of excess water. Leave for an hour, then rinse thoroughly and wipe dry with paper towels.

Put the ginger and chile into a small food processor and blend until smooth.

Heat the oil in a large pan and gently sauté the onion and garlic until soft. Stir in the ginger/chile paste and continue cooking for 2 minutes. Add the turmeric, coriander, cumin, and half the garam masala, and cook for another minute, stirring continuously. Add the tomatoes and continue cooking and stirring for 1 more minute.

Tip in the eggplants, turn down the heat and simmer, covered, until the dish resembles a purée—about 1 hour—adding a small amount of water if it seems as if it's drying out. Add the rest of the garam masala, stirring it in well for about 5 minutes. Check the seasoning and serve with nan and/or chapati.

Tabbouleh

Serves 4-6

1½ cups bulgur, rinsed,
  soaked in cold water for
  30 minutes, and
  thoroughly drained

1 large red onion, finely chopped

3 heaping tablespoons crushed
  walnuts

8 cherry tomatoes, cut in half

1 cucumber, peeled, seeded
  and chopped

2 tablespoons finely chopped
  flat-leaf parsley leaves

1 tablespoon finely chopped
  cilantro

2 tablespoons finely chopped
  mint leaves

Juice of 2 lemons

¼ cup extra-virgin olive oil

1 head of romaine lettuce

12 olives, a mixture of black and
  green, pitted and cut in half

Whole-wheat pita bread,
  for serving

There are as many recipes for tabbouleh among the Jews of the Middle East and north Africa as there are for colcannon among the Catholics of southern Ireland. Israeli Jews have adopted a style that has much more bulgur than other ingredients, whereas in other parts of the Middle East, especially Lebanon, it looks more like a green salad. This recipe is somewhere in the middle, with the added slightly bitter bite of walnuts.

Method Place the bulgur in a large bowl. Using a large spoon, mix in the onion and walnuts. Add the tomatoes, cucumber, parsley, cilantro, and mint, and stir again. Pour in the lemon juice and olive oil and mix well.

Arrange the lettuce leaves like the spokes of a wheel on a large platter and tip in the tabbouleh. Scatter the olives on top.

Serve with the pita bread.

Health note: Bulgur is a highly nutritious whole-grain cereal providing protein, fiber, and B vitamins. Made like this, tabbouleh overflows with heart-protective and cancer-preventative phytonutrients as well as the digestive benefits of mint and coriander leaves (cilantro).

Chopped herring with apple

Serves 4

2 salted herring fillets

2 pickled herring fillets

2 hard-boiled eggs, finely chopped

1 medium white onion, very finely chopped

1 apple, peeled, cored, and grated

2 tablespoons matzo meal

1 teaspoon brown sugar

2 tablespoons lemon juice

2 tablespoons cider vinegar

Ground white pepper

What could be more Jewish than chopped herring—one of the healthiest recipes brought from Eastern Europe? This dish may seem like a lot of work, but I promise you it's worth it: totally different from any commercial product. And if you're not Jewish and have never tasted this icon of kosher cooking, get chopping. And I mean chopping—not shoving it in a blender, where it loses its wonderful texture. This is a slightly healthier version of my Aunt Gertie's recipe, with much less sugar and no added salt, and is best eaten with traditional Jewish rye bread made with caraway seeds.

Method Put the fish on a large chopping board and chop until fine. Put into a serving bowl, add the eggs, onion, and apple, and mix well.

Sprinkle in the matzo meal and sugar, and mix again. Add the lemon juice and vinegar and stir well. Season to taste with ground white pepper.

Health note Herring simply oozes good health, as it's full of essential fatty acids for brain function, plus protein and lots of vitamin D, which is essential for strong bones; your body needs it in order to absorb calcium.

Schmaltz herrings

Serves 4

4 schmaltz or matjes herring fillets,
  cut into 1-inch slices

4 medium tomatoes, sliced

1 cucumber, peeled and sliced

1 small red onion, very finely
  sliced

Juice of 1 small lemon

1 tablespoon olive oil

Black pepper

1 tablespoon chopped fresh parsley

For European and American Jews, herring is probably the most important fish. Its popularity, which began in Eastern Europe and Germany, has been taken wherever these Jews migrated. For them, herring was never out of season, and when it was not available fresh, they devised many ways of preserving it so that this healthy fish could be eaten year-round.

When I was young, one of my many uncles owned a very famous kosher deli in Petticoat Lane, the heart of London's East End Jewish community. Most Sunday mornings I went there with my father and to this day I can close my eyes and smell that wonderful shop: wooden barrels full of pickled cucumbers, sacks of bagels hot from the bakery around the corner. While my father shopped, my treat was a bagel with schmaltz herring.

The traditional schmaltz herring is made from mature fish (which has a higher fat content), filleted and preserved in brine. The Dutch matjes herring is a younger fish, skinned, filleted and preserved in a mix of brine, sugar, and vinegar. Either way, this recipe makes a wonderfully delicious appetizer or light meal; as the latter, it was traditionally served with warm, boiled potatoes.

Method Arrange the fish, tomato, and cucumber slices alternately in a dish. Scatter the sliced onion on top.

Mix together the lemon juice, olive oil, and black pepper to taste, and pour them over the dish. Serve with the chopped parsley scattered on top.

Smoked white fish salad

Serves 4-6

2 pounds smoked whitefish
  (easily available in the US and in
  some fishmongers in the UK) or
  other smoked white fish, such as
  halibut or cod

1/4 cup live plain yogurt

1/4 cup mascarpone cheese

1 canteloupe, peeled,
  seeded and cut into cubes

2 celery stalks, finely chopped

1 small red onion, finely chopped

Juice of 1 lemon

1 butterhead lettuce

1/4 cup finely chopped chives

Smoking, salting, and sun-drying were the earliest methods of preserving fish, although pickling, suitable for oily fish like herring, became popular in Europe toward the end of the 19th century. Smoked salmon (lox), haddock, and kippers were appreciated in the UK, but salmon became the hallmark of Jews in London's East End. Smoked whitefish was never as important in the UK as it became in Europe or in the delis of New York.

I was given this wonderful, nutritious salad, very low in saturated fats and rich in everything else, in the London home of a Danish Jewish family, where it was made with smoked halibut.

Method Break the fish into bite-sized pieces. Mix together the yogurt and mascarpone cheese and carefully fold in the fish.

Put the cantaloupe, celery, and onion into a bowl. Add lemon juice to taste. Gently fold the fish into the salad. Arrange on individual plates on a bed of lettuce leaves.

Serve sprinkled with the chives.

Tuna roll

Serves 4

*14 ounces canned tuna in oil—about
  1 1/2 cups (undrained weight)*
*1/4 cups grated Parmesan
  cheese*
2 large eggs, well beaten
1 1/4 cups medium matzo meal
Mayonnaise, for serving

Until the Second World War, there was a large orthodox Jewish community in Rome. Its members combined typical Italian ingredients such as tuna and Parmesan cheese to make this version of the traditional boiled *gefilte* fish.

    Gefilte is the Yiddish word for filled or stuffed, and is used to describe many different dishes. The original fish balls used to be poached and served stuffed into the skin of the fish.

Method Put the tuna, with its oil, into a large bowl with the Parmesan cheese, eggs, and matzo meal. Mash well with a fork. Make into a sausage shape and wrap in cheesecloth or plastic wrap.

    Poach in a large pan of simmering water for 30 minutes, until set. Remove from the pan and chill. Serve sliced, with mayonnaise—preferably homemade, or use your own favorite commercial variety.

Health note This is a high-protein recipe which also contains calcium, B vitamins, and a relatively small proportion of carbohydrates.

Italian tuna toasts

Serves 6

One 6 ¼-ounce. can tuna in
   olive oil (undrained weight)
3 canned anchovy fillets,
   finely chopped
¼ cup (½ stick) unsalted butter,
   at room temperature, cubed
1 teaspoon chopped fresh oregano
   (dried won't do)
Juice and zest of 1 lemon
Black pepper
1 standard ciabatta loaf, sliced
   lengthwise and each half cut
   into three pieces
Peeled cucumber
Mixed black and green pitted olives

Olives and ciabatta make this unmistakably a dish of Italy, where it has long been a favorite of the Jewish community. This delicious appetizer will work with mackerel or any canned or chunky smoked fish. Serve with peeled cucumber with mixed black and green pitted olives

Method Put the tuna, with its oil, into a food-processor and whizz until it breaks up. Add the anchovies, butter, oregano, and lemon zest and whizz until smooth. Season to taste with lemon juice and black pepper.

   Toast the ciabatta pieces and pile the tuna mixture on top. Mix together the cucumber and olives and serve on the side.

Health note The essential fatty acids from the fish are not only good brain food, but may also help with problems such as attention deficit hyperactivity disorder (ADHD) and dyslexia. This dish is a good source of vitamin D, which is important for the prevention of osteoporosis as it improves the absorption of calcium.

Trout and mushroom piroshki

Serves 6-8

4 tablespoons olive oil

1 onion, finely chopped

4 ounces trout fillet, cut into thin
strips along the grain of the fish
(about 1/2 cup)

4 ounces wild mushrooms, heads
only, wiped clean and finely
chopped (about 1 heaping cup)

1/2 cup vegetable broth–
see recipe for Barley with
mushrooms and marjoram
(page 47) or use a good-quality,
low-salt stock cube or
bouillon powder

1 sprig each of thyme, rosemary
and parsley

1 1/2 cups crème fraîche
(if unavailable, use sour cream)

1 heaping tablespoon chopped
fresh dill

1 heaping tablespoon finely
chopped chives

18 ounces frozen vegetarian
pie dough, thoroughly thawed
(or if homemade, enough pie
dough for two 8-inch pies)

Nothing could be more authentically Ashkenazi than this Russian *piroshki*. Unlike the New York Jewish street food, which was traditionally a bite-sized snack (known there as a *knish*), this is a large wrap covered in pastry dough and is equally delicious hot or cold.

Surprisingly, the first time I ate this dish I wasn't at home, but at one of many memorable meals I enjoyed with my father in one of his favorite restaurants. A Jewish white Russian émigré friend served it in its traditional Russian form as *koulibiac* every Friday night in his London restaurant. There, it was made with a whole salmon.

Method Preheat the oven to 400°F. Heat 2 tablespoons of the oil in a large pan and gently sauté the onion until soft. Place the sautéed onion and oil in a bowl. Put the remaining 2 tablespoons of oil in the pan, heat it, and add the trout. Fry gently until it turns whitish–about 20 seconds. Add the fish to the onion.

Strain the onion-and-trout juices back into the pan, heat them, and add the mushrooms, broth and thyme, rosemary, and parsley. Simmer for 3 minutes. Fish out the mushrooms and add them to the onion and trout. Strain the broth, then pour it back into the pan and reduce over a high heat until you have about 1 tablespoon left. Stir in the crème fraîche, onion, trout, mushrooms, dill, and chives.

Roll out the pastry dough and cut into 4-inch circles. Brush the edges with water. Put about a tablespoon of the mixture in the center of each circle, fold the dough over, and seal the edges. Bake for 20 minutes.

Health note Scientists have now proved the truth of the old saying that fish is good for the brain. All oily fish provide essential fatty acids which improve brain function and protect the central nervous system.

Warm smoked salmon with raspberries

Serves 2-3

10 ounces smoked salmon (lox),
cut in 1 thick slice

1/4 cup balsamic vinegar

1 bunch watercress

1/2 fennel bulb, thinly sliced
lengthwise

1 small carton raspberries (about
20 fruits)

Black pepper

Wasabi (a hot green paste made
from Japanese sea cabbage)

1 lemon, quartered

This recipe came from a Jewish friend who worked for some years in Japan. It's his adaptation of sushi, which, thanks to the oily fish, makes a healthy, high-protein appetizer that is so attractive to look at. Wasabi has a wonderful hot and sweet flavor and is also believed to have cancer-fighting properties. How different can you get from the traditional plate of smoked salmon?

Method Cut the smoked salmon into strips about an inch long. Put into a small, wide pan along with the balsamic vinegar and heat gently, stirring lightly, for 1 minute. Remove from the heat.

On individual plates, make mounds of the watercress, then the fennel, then the raspberries. Arrange the warm smoked salmon strips on top. Pour the warm balsamic vinegar over them. Give each dish a twist of black pepper. Put a generous teaspoon of wasabi on the side of each plate.

Serve garnished with the lemon quarters.

Greek chicken patties

Serves 6

4 skinned boneless chicken breasts—or use meat left over from making Chicken soup with matzo dumplings (see page 66)

1 medium onion, quartered

3 teaspoons chopped fresh dill or fennel fronds

3 tablespoons fine matzo meal

3 eggs, well beaten

About 1/2 cup olive oil

1 iceberg lettuce, finely sliced

There have been Jews in Greece since ancient times. As happened wherever Jews settled, they adapted local ingredients and cooking styles to the laws of kosher eating. These patties are equally delicious cold, make good party canapés, and they're an ideal healthy food to include in children's lunchboxes.

Method If using uncooked chicken breasts, cut them into slivers and poach in a little seasoned water until tender—about 5 minutes. Grind the chicken with the onion in a food-processor or put through a meat grinder. Put into a bowl and mix well. Add the dill or fennel, matzo meal and eggs, and mix well again.

Wet your hands and, taking a large spoonful at a time, mold into small patties.

Heat the olive oil until nearly smoking. Sauté the patties gently in the oil, turning once, until golden. Cool slightly and serve on the lettuce.

Health note Full of protein, B vitamins, and minerals, these patties are low in saturated fats. The dill or fennel makes them extremely easy to digest,

Chicken livers with grapes

Serves 2-3

2 tablespoons olive oil

2 shallots, very finely chopped (if unavailable, use 2 tablespoons chopped mild onions)

12 ounces chicken livers (fresh are best, but frozen will do), all membranes removed (about 1 1/2 cups)

About 3 tablespoons flour

1/4 cup red wine

12 seedless grapes (red or white), cut in half

2-3 slices toast

2 tablespoons finely chopped parsley

The traditional Jewish cook had the typical peasant approach to a chicken: nothing was wasted. The feet, neck, and giblets were all used in one way or another, as was the liver. Rather than the ubiquitous chopped liver, however, why not try this quick and healthy recipe popular with the Jewish community in the south of France?

Method Heat the oil in a pan and sauté the shallots gently until soft. Cut the chicken livers into bite-sized pieces, if necessary, and roll in the flour. Add to the pan and cook, stirring continuously, until cooked right through—about 5 minutes. Pour in the wine, bring to a boil, then turn the heat down to low.

Add the grapes and continue cooking gently to warm through—about 2 minutes. Put the mixture onto the toast and sprinkle with the parsley.

Health note This dish is particularly beneficial for women. It's a wonderful source of iron and vitamin B12, the vital ingredients to prevent anemia and make healthy blood. During their child-bearing years, most women hover on the borderline of anemia and are likely to have very low stores of iron.

Chicken liver pâté with pistachio nuts

Serves 4

2 tablespoons olive oil

1 medium onion, finely chopped

10 ounces chicken livers
   (defrosted frozen livers will do),
   all membranes removed
   (about 1 1/4 cups)

2 hard-boiled eggs, peeled

2 tablespoons pistachio nuts,
   roughly crushed

The use of nuts and nut oils is common in all Sephardi cooking, and in Mediterranean areas olive oil is an everyday staple. Pistachios, although grown throughout the Mediterranean, were a particular favorite of the Persian Jews; in fact, the name comes from *pistakion*, the ancient Greek corruption of the Persian word *pistah*.

Method Heat the oil in a frying pan, add the onion, and sauté gently until soft. Meanwhile, broil the chicken livers until well done. Mix the livers with the onion in the pan, then put the frying pan contents (including the oil) into a blender or food-processor. Add the eggs and whizz until smooth.

Pour into a bowl, add the pistachio nuts, and mix gently but well. Spoon the pâté into a small attractive dish, smooth the top, and chill for at least 3 hours.

Health note This version of chicken liver pâté is rich in protein, iron, and B vitamins from the liver. Thanks to the oil and nuts, it also contains substantial amounts of monounsaturated fats, which help reduce cholesterol levels, a benefit aided and abetted by the onion.

Sweet salami salad

Serves 6-8

1 1/3 cups cooked rice (preferably a
   mixture of white and wild)

1/2 cup fresh or defrosted
   frozen corn

2 scallions, finely chopped

1 pickled cucumber, rinsed
   and chopped

3 ounces lowish-fat salami, cut
   into cubes (about 1/2 cup)

For the dressing

2/3 cup extra-virgin olive oil

1/4 cup white wine vinegar

1 strong scallion, very
   finely chopped

2 pinches of dry mustard

1/2 teaspoon organic brown sugar

Kosher salami is usually made from beef, though veal is sometimes used. It's nearly always flavored with garlic, although in Latin America they use chili, while Eastern Europe favors paprika. In Holland, they eat an unusual salami that isn't cooked or smoked, but more like steak tartare in a sausage skin. One of my favorites is a beef and garlic salami which has been smoked, then air-dried.

This is typical foodstuff of the Jews from Italy and the mountain regions of Germany and Switzerland. As it's a fairly hard salami, you can slice it very thinly and it tends to have less fat than its non-kosher equivalents.

Method Mix the salad ingredients together in a bowl.

Put all the dressing ingredients into a large measuring cup and whisk well. Pour the dressing over the salad to serve.

Kiddush cup This cup would have been used for the blessing over wine at the Sabbath and at the beginning of every festival. There are two scenes from the life of Abraham embossed on the coconut goblet: the three angels visiting Abraham to announce the birth of Isaac (center left), the binding of Isaac (far right). There is also a scene from the life of Joseph: men drinking (far left). The stem and base (see also page 160) are made from rosewood and the cup was made in England in 1803. It is very likely that the man who commissioned it would have been called Abraham.

soups

Lemon and egg

Serves 6

8 cups chicken broth,
preferably homemade—see
recipe for Chicken soup with
matzo dumplings (page 66)
or use a good-quality, low-salt
cube or bouillon powder
1 cup long-grain rice
4 egg yolks
1 heaping tablespoon flour
Juice of 3 lemons
1 tablespoon finely chopped parsley

There have been Jews in Greece since classical times. Although, tragically, virtually the whole community was wiped out in the latter stages of the Second World War, they had been masters of adapting the Jewish dietary laws to the traditional regional food of their adopted country.

This light, nourishing, and easily digestible broth was a favorite recipe used when breaking the fast of Yom Kippur (the Day of Atonement).

Method Bring the broth to a boil, add the rice, and cook until just tender—about 12 minutes.

Meanwhile, in the top pan of a double boiler over gently simmering water, cream the egg yolks and beat in the flour. Add the lemon juice and heat the mixture, stirring continuously, until it just starts to thicken. Gradually add some of the broth, a tablespoon at a time, continuing to stir until you have a thin paste. Pour the egg mixture back into the broth and rice, and heat gently, being careful not to let it boil.

Season to taste and serve sprinkled with parsley.

Spinach with yogurt

Serves 4

2 tablespoons unsalted butter
1 large garlic clove, very
finely chopped
8 ounces baby spinach
(about 6 cups)
1 tablespoon fresh mint,
finely chopped
4 cups live plain yogurt
1 teaspoon crushed caraway seeds
Paprika, for serving
4 small sprigs of mint, for serving

One of the great joys of Greek food is the variety of regional cooking with its subtle local influences. It's not surprising, then, that the dishes of Greek Jews reflect this wonderful diverse cuisine.

This soup, from Crete, includes the universal Greek favorites, spinach and yogurt, with added paprika as an indication of its Ottoman origins.

Method Put the butter into a large pot. Add the garlic and sauté gently for 2 minutes.

Wash the spinach thoroughly and add to the pot with only the water still clinging to it. Add the mint. Cover and steam slowly, shaking the pot every 30 seconds or so, until the spinach is wilted—about 5 minutes.

Put the yogurt into another pan with the caraway seeds. Heat through, but don't boil. Add the spinach and its juices and stir well.

Serve sprinkled sparingly with paprika and decorated with mint sprigs.

Barley with mushrooms and marjoram

Serves 4-6

For the broth

You can use good-quality, low-salt kosher vegetable stock cubes or bouillon powder, but this home-made broth is infinitely better.

2 onions, 1 quartered, 1 left whole

2 large carrots, cut into large chunks

1 fennel bulb, quartered

1 large leek, cut into large chunks

1 turnip, quartered

4 large mushrooms, quartered

2 celery stalks, cut into large chunks

6 bay leaves

1 large sprig of sage

2 sprigs of thyme

1 sprig of rosemary

10 black peppercorns

For the soup

3 tablespoons sunflower or canola (rapeseed) oil

2 leeks, white parts only, finely chopped

1 garlic clove, finely chopped

2/3 cup barley, thoroughly washed

2 bay leaves

4 cups vegetable broth (see above)

1 carrot, finely chopped

4 ounces mushrooms, with stalks, finely chopped (about 1 heaping cup)

4 large sprigs of fresh marjoram (or oregano) or 1 level teaspoon either dried herb

1 1/4 cups sour cream

1 small bunch of chives, chopped

My mother's eldest sister, Ada, was married to a taciturn, fierce Polish tailor whose heavily accented English was difficult to understand—especially for my cousins and me as we were growing up. They lived in Willesden, north London, in a house filled with dark, heavy furniture and thick curtains that always used to be closed. It was one of the few places where the family gathered where the children had to sit quietly and be on their best behavior for fear of upsetting Uncle Henry. Ada was a wonderful cook and we nearly always had this soup: a traditional Ashkenazi Polish recipe. Henry always complained that it never tasted like his mother's version. But I loved it then and you'll love it now.

Method First, make the broth by putting all the broth ingredients in a large pot. Add about 6 cups of water. Bring to a boil and simmer, uncovered, for 1 hour. Strain, pushing the vegetable pulp through a wire mesh strainer with a wooden spoon.

To make the soup, melt the oil in a large pot and gently sauté the leeks and garlic until soft but not brown. Add the barley, bay leaves, and broth, and simmer until the barley is tender—about 40 minutes. Add the carrot, mushrooms, and marjoram (or oregano) and simmer until the carrots are tender. Discard the bay leaves and any woody herb stalks. Season and stir in the sour cream, reserving one spoonful for each bowl to be used as a topping.

Serve with a dollop of sour cream and the chives scattered on top.

Ajo blanco

Serves 6

3 tablespoons extra-virgin olive oil

8 large garlic cloves, very finely
  chopped

2 1/2 cups ground almonds

3 cups fresh white bread crumbs

2 1/4 cups white grape juice

1 cup live plain yogurt

16 seedless black grapes, cut in half

I'm not sure whether I was more impressed by the synagogue or this amazing soup the first time I visited Cádiz, in southern Spain, with my very dear friend John Belmont—sadly, no longer with us. Fleeing the Nazi occupation of Belgium as a young boy, John had walked his way through Europe; he managed to get to Spain and finally settled in London. He spoke several languages, was a wonderful raconteur and had an uncanny Jewish nose for good food. After seeing the synagogue, he sniffed out a tiny side-street café and insisted that we start with this soup.

Imagine my surprise when what I assumed were black olives floating on the top turned out to be sweet grapes, which contrasted wonderfully with the sharp flavor of garlic. Thanks to the garlic, this is heart protection in a bowl.

Method Mix together the oil, garlic, and almonds. Put into a blender with half the bread crumbs, half the grape juice, and a cup of water. Whizz until smooth and pour into a large bowl.

Put the remaining grape juice and bread crumbs, the yogurt, and another cup of water into the blender and whizz until smooth. Combine the two mixtures, stir well, and chill.

Serve with the grapes on the side or floating on top.

Sweet and sour tomatoes with noodles

Serves 4

6 large tomatoes

2 tablespoons tomato paste

Juice of 1 medium lemon

2 tablespoons raw sugar
    (if unavailable use, use
    light brown sugar)

5 cups chicken broth,
    preferably homemade—see
    recipe for Chicken soup with
    matzo dumplings (page 66)
    or use a good-quality, low-salt
    cube or bouillon powder

3 ounces dried rice noodles

In parts of the Middle East, such as ancient Persia, Morocco, and Iraq, as well as in the Far East and China, Jews developed a taste for sweet-and-sour dishes. These have become a hallmark of much Sephardi cooking.

All soups really do taste better when prepared with homemade broth, but it's particularly worth the extra effort for this delicately flavored dish. Of course, you can make it with vegetable broth (see recipe for Barley with mushrooms and marjoram on page 47) if you're planning it as part of a non-meat meal.

Method Put the tomatoes into a blender and whizz until completely broken down. Put them in a large pot along with the tomato paste, lemon juice, sugar, and broth. Simmer for 25 minutes.

Add the noodles and continue simmering until the noodles are cooked—usually about 5 minutes, but check the package instructions. Adjust the seasoning and serve..

Health note This soup is exceptionally rich in the important carotenoid lycopene (in the tomatoes and tomato paste), which is specifically protective against prostate cancer, breast cancer, and eye problems.

Potato soup

Serves 4-6

1/4 cup olive oil

1 pound Russet or yellow potatoes,
   peeled and chopped, about
   2 1/2 cups

2 large carrots, peeled
   and chopped

1 medium onion, very finely sliced

1 garlic clove, very finely chopped

About 1 cup milk

1 teaspoon ground fennel seeds

4 cups live plain yogurt

4 sprigs of dill, for garnish

Greek cooking had its own classical origins, but was heavily influenced by the neighboring Balkans, Turks, and the many nations with which the Greeks traded. Jews settling in Greece borrowed from all these cooking styles.

Method Heat the oil in a large pan and gently sauté the potatoes, carrots, onion, and garlic until soft but not brown—about 10 minutes. Add just enough milk to cover and simmer until soft—about 15 minutes. Mix the fennel seeds with the yogurt and heat gently in another pan, being careful not to let it boil. Add the vegetables to the yogurt mixture and warm through.

   If you want a smooth soup, blend it and warm through again. Serve with the dill sprigs on top.

Health note This soup is a good source of energy, and is low in fat and rich in carotenoids from the carrots. It also contains heart-protective phytochemicals from the onions and garlic, and lots of calcium from the milk and yogurt. The fennel seeds improve digestion and ensure that you get the most out of every spoonful.

Cream of jerusalem artichoke

Serves 4

1 skinless chicken breast, shredded
   along the grain of the meat

2 tablespoons olive oil

1 pound Jerusalem artichokes

4 cups chicken broth,
   preferably homemade—see
   recipe for Chicken soup with
   matzo dumplings (page 66)
   or use a good-quality, low-salt
   cube or bouillon powder

1/4 cup finely chopped
   flat-leaf parsley

Jerusalem artichokes have nothing to do with Jerusalem. Their name is a corruption of the Italian word *girasole*, which means "sunflower," to which these delicious little tubers are related. In this soup, their unique flavor is combined with protein, and vitamin-rich chicken to make a nourishing and unusual soup that is just as good cold as hot.

Method Stir-fry the chicken pieces in the olive oil and reserve. Simmer the Jerusalem artichokes in the broth until tender—about 15 minutes. Whizz in a blender or food processor until smooth. Put back into a large pot, add the chicken, and reheat gently.

   Serve sprinkled with parsley.

Health note Jerusalem artichokes are rich in inulin, which isn't broken down during digestion and ends up in the large intestine, where it provides food for the beneficial probiotic bacteria.

White beans with pasta and Swiss chard

Serves 6-8

5 tablespoons olive oil

1 small onion, finely chopped

2 garlic cloves, finely chopped

1 carrot, finely chopped

1 stalk celery, finely sliced

8 ounces Swiss chard or rainbow chard, leaves separated from the stalks, but both reserved

8 cups vegetable broth—
  see recipe for Barley with mushrooms and marjoram (page 47) or use a good-quality, low-salt cube or bouillon powder

12 ounces (about 2 1/4 cups) canned cannellini or other white bean (drained weight), rinsed and drained

9 ounces (about 4 cups) small pasta such as rotini or bow ties (or farfel: small, grain-like pieces of toasted pasta)

About 6 tablespoons grated Parmesan cheese

This is a kosher adaptation of the great Italian peasant soup, *pasta e fagioli*, and it's closer to the Naples version, which is made with olive oil instead of the butter and pancetta used in other parts of Italy. You can always omit the Parmesan if you're serving this as part of a meat meal.

With lots of protein and heart-protective natural chemicals in the beans, and the amazing content of beta carotene and other vital carotenoids in the chard, this soup is a substantial and nourishing meal on its own.

Method Put the oil into a large pot and gently sauté the onion, garlic, carrot, celery, and chard stalks for about 10 minutes. Add the broth and bring to a boil. Add the beans to the soup and return to a boil. After 2 minutes, add the torn green chard leaves and cook for another 3-4 minutes until the beans are tender. Keep warm.

Cook the pasta according to the package instructions. Drain and add to the bean mixture. Serve sprinkled with Parmesan cheese.

Tomatoes with peppers

Serves 4

8 large scallions, finely chopped

2 garlic cloves, finely chopped

3 tablespoons olive oil

4 large red peppers, seeded
*   and finely chopped*

2 large tomatoes, coarsely chopped

4 cups vegetable broth—
*   see recipe for Barley with*
*   mushrooms and marjoram*
*   (page 47) or use a good-quality,*
*   low-salt cube or bouillon powder*

2 large sprigs of thyme

1 large sprig of rosemary

There doesn't seem to be any evidence of Jews in South America until the 16th century, so it's unlikely that any Jewish cook came into contact with tomatoes before then. Tomatoes were first introduced to Europe by the Spanish in the 1700s, and they soon spread throughout the Mediterranean into north Africa and the Middle East. As members of the nightshade family of plants, they weren't popular to begin with—people were afraid to eat them because of their deadly relative. But it wasn't long before they were embraced by all cooks—Jewish, Muslim, and Christian.

Method Gently sauté the onions and garlic in the oil until softened but not brown. Add the peppers and tomatoes and continue to cook for 5 minutes, stirring continuously. Add the broth and herbs, bring to a boil, and simmer until the peppers are tender—about 10 minutes.

Remove the woody herb stalks and whizz the soup in a blender or food-processor until smooth. Serve hot or chilled.

Health note Combined here in the Mediterranean favorites of garlic, peppers, thyme, and rosemary, the health benefits of this dish are powerfully protective and nourishing—but you'll enjoy it simply for its taste.

Quick borscht

Serves 4-6

2 pounds fresh beets, peeled and cubed, about 4 1/2–5 1/2 cups

1 medium turnip, cubed

2 celery stalks, coarsely chopped

2 garlic cloves

2 carrots, coarsely chopped

3 tablespoons olive oil

4 cups vegetable broth–
see recipe for Barley with mushrooms and marjoram (page 47) or use a good-quality, low-salt cube or bouillon powder

1 cup live plain yogurt

Juice of 1 lemon

Beets are one of the greatest of health-giving vegetables. They were revered by the ancient Greeks, used by the Romanies as a blood-building medicine, and are given to convalescent patients in Russia, Poland, and most of Eastern Europe to this day. In traditional medicine, beets have been used as a treatment for leukemia and anemia, and modern science has discovered specific anticarcinogens in this vegetable's red coloring.

Not all of the Ashkenazi cooking from Eastern Europe is instant heart attack on a plate, and this recipe is not only delicious (hot or cold), but a provider of great nutritional benefits, too. My mother always served this with sour cream, but yogurt contains far less fat. If she wanted to serve borscht with a meat meal, she would leave out the sour cream and thicken it with beaten egg yolk. I prefer to use soy yogurt.

Method Put the beets, turnip, celery, garlic, and carrots into a food processor and whizz them finely.

Put the oil into a large pot and gently sauté the vegetables, stirring continuously, for 5 minutes. Pour in the broth and simmer for 30 minutes. Strain into a clean pot and return to a simmer.

Mix the yogurt and lemon juice well. Serve the soup in individual bowls with a swirl of yogurt sauce on top.

Zucchini soup with dolcelatte

Serves 4

1 onion, finely chopped

1 leek, finely chopped
  (if unavailable, use 1 1/4 cups
  chopped mild onion)

3 tablespoons olive oil

4 smallish zucchini, finely sliced

2 1/2 cups vegetable broth—see
  recipe for Barley with
  mushrooms and marjoram (page
  47) or use a good quality, low-salt
  stock cube or bouillon powder

2 cups low-fat milk

7 ounces dolcelatte cheese (or
  Gorgonzola or other blue-veined
  cheese)—about 2 cups

When I was growing up in the small Hertfordshire town of Tring, nearly all my schoolfriends were Christian. It wasn't many years before I tasted the traditional British Christmas leftover favorite, Brussels sprouts and Stilton soup. When I was a student living in London, I met a Jewish girl whose family had been expelled from Egypt. Her mother was Italian, and imagine my surprise when, invited to eat with them, she served this wonderful soup which she said was her grandmother's recipe from Rome! The taste took me instantly back to my childhood in Tring and reminded me, even then, that food is a great way to build bridges between people.

Method In a pot large enough to hold a couple of quarts, gently sauté the onion and leek in the oil until soft but not brown. Add the zucchini, broth, and milk. Bring to a boil and simmer very gently until the zucchini is tender—about 10 minutes.

Whizz in a blender or food processor until smooth. Return to the pot and bring back to a simmer. Crumble in the cheese and stir until dissolved.

Health note Leeks, like onions and garlic, help to lower cholesterol and protect against infection; the skin of zucchini is rich in beta carotene; and the milk and cheese provide protein and lots of calcium for strong bones.

Avocado cream

Serves 4-6

6 scallions, very finely chopped

1 garlic clove, very finely chopped

3 tablespoons olive oil

2 heaping tablespoons flour

4 cups low-fat milk

1 large or 2 small ripe avocados

1 egg yolk

1/2 cup live plain yogurt

1/4 cup chopped fresh chives

For 8,000 years, the indigenous peoples of South America have eaten avocados and used the rest of the tree—leaves, rind, seeds, and bark—as medicines. Israel is one of the world's major growers of avocados, and this delicious soup is a great way to enjoy their benefits.

Method Gently sauté the onions and garlic in the olive oil until softened but not brown. Remove from the heat and sprinkle in the flour, stirring continuously until well blended. Return to the heat and cook gently until well combined and thickened. Still stirring, gradually add the milk.

Mash the avocado(s) and add to the pan immediately. Heat through, stirring continuously. Mix together the egg yolk and yogurt and add to the pan. Warm through gently; don't allow it to boil.

Serve warm with the chives sprinkled on top.

Health note This is a super-nutrient food, rich in mono-unsaturated fats to reduce cholesterol and with significant amounts of oleic acid, an antioxidant that protects against some cancers, and against strokes and heart disease.

Summer berries

Serves 4

2 pounds mixed summer berries
(about 6–8 cups)
Juice of ¹/₂ lemon
1 tablespoon honey
1 teaspoon ground cinnamon
1 heaped teaspoon arrowroot
(if unavailable, use cornstarch)
4 tablespoons live plain yogurt

Here's another fruit soup which has been traditionally eaten for generations in Eastern Europe, especially in Hungary, where they grow wonderful summer berries. Although cooked, the fruit will still provide good amounts of vitamin C as there's so much there to start with.

Method Put the fruit, lemon juice, honey, and cinnamon into a large pot with 3 cups water. Simmer until the fruit is soft. Push it through a fine mesh strainer with a wooden spoon and return it to the pan.

Mix the arrowroot with a little water to make a firm paste. Add to the pan, mix it in, and bring slowly to a boil, stirring continuously.

Serve cold, with a spoonful of yogurt in each bowl. (If keeping kosher, omit the yogurt if serving as part of a meat meal.)

Health note All the dark berries are among the richest sources of the protective ORAC antioxidant units (see page 13). As a bonus, the most recent research shows that cinnamon can help regulate blood-sugar levels and prevent type-2 diabetes.

Red grapes with nuts

Serves 4

8 ounces (about 1 1/2 cups)
   red grapes

2 cups live plain yogurt

2 1/2 cups low-fat milk

2 tablespoons honey

1/4 cup ground walnuts

Grated zest of 1 lemon

1 teaspoon vanilla extract

8 walnut halves

Chilled fruit soups are an enormous source of vitamin C as they're often uncooked, so none of this nutrient is lost. Most Jewish cookbooks include at least one fruit soup, and they're a traditional favorite in Eastern Europe, Russia, Germany, and Israel. Melon soup is popular in Russia, red cherry in Hungary, and every imaginable fruit soup is to be found in Israel.

Although wine is an integral part of Jewish religious practice, alcohol has never featured largely in Jewish social life. Historically, I think these soups were used in place of bitter aperitifs as an appetite stimulant.

Method   Push the grapes through a fine mesh strainer with a wooden spoon.

Whisk the yogurt, milk, and honey together and mix in the grape pulp. Stir in the ground walnuts, lemon zest, and vanilla extract. Serve chilled with the walnut halves floating on top.

Health note In this recipe, there are all the protective properties of the antioxidants in grapes combined with the cholesterol-lowering monounsaturated fats in the walnuts.

Indian cod and chickpea soup

Serves 4

4 plum tomatoes

2 large red peppers

About 5 tablespoons olive oil

4 shallots, each cut into 8 pieces

2 garlic cloves, finely chopped

1 small fennel bulb, finely sliced

2 red chiles, seeded and
   finely sliced

1 teaspoon ground turmeric

1/2 teaspoon ground cumin

4 cups fish or vegetable broth

10 ounces cod fillet, in small pieces,
   about 1 1/4 cups

9 ounces, drained weight (about
   1 2/3 cups), canned chickpeas,
   drained and rinsed

3 tablespoons finely chopped
   mixed parsley, cilantro and mint

Juice of 1 small lemon

My mother used to make fish soup, but refused to use the eels which my Dutch father said were acceptable to most Dutch Jews. Nice though her version was, it was also a bit weak and feeble. If only she'd known an Indian Jewish family, her fish soup would have been like this hot, spicy, and substantial dish! Full of protein, fiber, and protective antioxidants, it is a health feast as well as a taste delight.

Method   Preheat the oven to 425°F. Roast the tomatoes and peppers for about 30 minutes, until charred. When they're cool enough to handle, rub the skins off the peppers, and seed and cut them into strips. Quarter the tomatoes.

Put the oil into a large pot and gently sauté the shallots and garlic for 3 minutes. Add the fennel and chiles and continue cooking for another 3 minutes. Sprinkle in the turmeric and cumin. Stir well and cook for 2 minutes. Add the broth and bring to a simmer. Add the fish, chickpeas, peppers, tomatoes, and 2 tablespoons of the herbs, and continue simmering gently until the fish is cooked—about 10 minutes.

Sprinkle with the lemon juice, and the remaining herbs, and serve.

Fish with watercress

Serves 6

For the stock

You can use good-quality, low-salt kosher fish stock cubes or fish or vegetable bouillon powder, but this homemade stock is infinitely better.

4 ounces fish trimmings and bones

3 carrots, coarsely chopped

2 white onions,coarsely chopped

1 leek, coarsely chopped

1 sprig of rosemary

6 large sprigs of parsley

1 large sprig of mint

3 large sprigs of tarragon

8 white peppercorns

$1/2$ teaspoon salt

For the soup

18 ounces (about 2–2 $1/2$ cups) firm white-fish fillets (e.g. cod, halibut, haddock), cut into very fine strips along the grain of the flesh

$1/2$ teaspoon sea salt or kosher salt

$1/2$ teaspoon ginger paste or finely grated ginger

$1/4$ cup sherry

6 cups fish stock (see above)

3 teaspoons light soy sauce

1 teaspoon raw sugar (or regular sugar)

2 large bunches watercress, leaves stripped from the stalks

6 scallions, trimmed and cut diagonally

Here's another sweet-and-sour recipe, this time from the Far East. My cousin, Ann, trained as a nurse in London and went to work in America, where she met her future husband. Ira, a psychologist with the American military, was posted to the Far East, where they got married, and Ann sent me this recipe from a friend she met through the local rabbi.

Serve with rice cakes and a mixed salad and you have a perfect light lunch or supper.

Method To make the stock, put all the stock ingredients into a large pot and add 8 cups of water. Bring to a boil and simmer for 30 minutes. Strain through a fine mesh strainer or cheesecloth.

To make the soup, sprinkle the fish with sea salt. Mix the ginger paste with half the sherry, pour it over the fish, and let marinate for about 30 minutes.

Bring the stock to a boil and add the soy sauce, sugar, and the remaining sherry. Put the watercress leaves into a large bowl, with the fish on top. Ensuring that the stock is still boiling, pour it into the bowl, and leave it for 10 minutes. Serve sprinkled with the scallions on top.

Health note With absolutely no fat, lots of protein, iodine, and other minerals from the fish, huge cancer-fighting benefits from the watercress, and the energizing stimulation from the ginger, this soup is exceptionally healthy.

Smoked haddock and smoked salmon

Serves 4

1/4 cup (1/2 stick) unsalted butter

1 onion, finely chopped

2 1/2 cups low-fat milk

3 bay leaves

1/2 teaspoon ground nutmeg

10 ounces potatoes, cut into
  1/2-inch cubes (about 1 3/4–2 cups)

12 ounces undyed smoked
  haddock, skin removed, and
  broken along the grain into
  bite-sized pieces, about 1 1/2 cups

1 cup low-fat crème
  fraîche or heavy cream

4 ounces smoked salmon (lox),
  cut into strips, about 1/2 cup

Black pepper

Dill fronds, for serving

British Jews were no different from those who spread to the far-flung corners of the earth as they also adapted their food to available ingredients. I discovered how regional these adaptations were when staying with a Jewish family in Glasgow who were friends of my parents.

I was expecting smoked salmon, but not this wonderful variation of the traditional Scottish cullen skink. It is healthier made with low-fat crème fraîche, but forty years ago there was no alternative to the heavy cream that made it so unashamedly rich. I've persuaded myself that the benefits of oily fish and the total lack of fat in the haddock balance out the cream. My wife still makes it; sometimes we're very good, sometimes we aren't.

Method Melt the butter in a large saucepan and gently sauté the onion until soft but not brown. Pour in the milk, add the bay leaves, nutmeg, and potatoes, and simmer until the potatoes are just starting to become tender—about 10 minutes. Add the smoked haddock and simmer until cooked—about 7 minutes. Lift out the fish. Remove and discard the bay leaves.

Mash the potatoes thoroughly. Return the fish to the pan and add the crème fraîche or cream. Season to taste with pepper. Bring quickly to a boil, remove from the heat, and add the smoked salmon.

Serve hot with the dill fronds floating on top.

Spiced lamb soup

For the stock

You can use good-quality, low-salt kosher lamb stock cubes or bouillon powder, but this home-made stock is infinitely better.

2 pounds lamb bones, sawn into
  1 1/2-inch pieces

2 large red onions, coarsely chopped

2 large carrots, coarsely chopped

1 leek, coarsely chopped

2 celery stalks, coarsely chopped

1 large bunch of sage

1 sprig of rosemary

5 bay leaves

10 black peppercorns

For the soup

1 1/2 pounds stewing lamb, cubed

8 cups lamb stock (see above)

2 medium zucchinis, cut into
  thick slices

2 heaping tablespoons tomato paste

6 shallots, quartered

3 garlic cloves, finely chopped

1/2 teaspoon ground turmeric

1/2 teaspoon caraway seeds

1 saffron strand

Isolated and cut off from the rest of world's Jewry for 2,000 years, the Jews of Ethiopia are an extraordinary people. Unaffected by the rabbinical interpretations of the laws of kosher cooking, theirs is a style of food that is probably much closer to that of the biblical Jews than anything we eat today. Surviving as they did in the harsh climate of Ethiopia and often in difficult circumstances, to them meat was probably a luxury; when they had it, nothing was wasted. Like the Indians, Ethiopian Jews used pieces of large, flat bread to pick up their food. Also like the Indians, they had a taste for hot spices.

This recipe calls for lamb stock, but exactly the same method can be used to make beef stock, which also features in many of the recipes in this book.

Method First, make the stock. Preheat the oven to 425°F. Roast the bones for 30 minutes. Then put them, along with any meat still left clinging, into a large pot. Add the remaining stock ingredients and 3 quarts (12 cups) of water. Bring to a boil and simmer for 4 hours, regularly skimming off any fat. Strain through cheesecloth. Cover, leave until cold, and remove any remaining fat.

To make the soup, put all ingredients into a large pot. Bring to a boil and simmer for 2 hours, regularly skimming off any fat.

Health note This soup is a westernized adaptation of a traditional nourishing and sustaining dish, with the added protection against stomach cancer provided by the turmeric.

Lentils with meatballs

Serves 4

12 ounces (a heaping 1 3/4 cups)
   green lentils, rinsed and soaked
   in cold water for at least 2 hours
   (or according to the package
   instructions)

2 small onions, very finely chopped

2 garlic cloves, very finely chopped

1 small fennel bulb, very finely
   chopped

2 carrots, finely chopped

2 large tomatoes, coarsely chopped

2 tablespoons tomato paste

1 large sprig of rosemary

1 large sprig of thyme

2 bay leaves

12 ounces (1 1/2 cups) lean ground
   beef or lamb

Olive oil

1/4 cup chopped flat-leaf parsley

In many parts of the world, and at different times in their history, Jewish communities prospered. But to me they seem never to have lost the survival instincts which come from their history of traveling the wilderness, enslavement, bondage, and persecution. This made their women frugal cooks who helped their families survive on the most meager of resources.

In terms of nutritional value for the money, there's little to compare with lentils and all their relatives, and the Jewish housewives adapted them, whether they were making *dhal* in India, Kurdish dishes in Iraq, or soups and stews throughout the Mediterranean. Jews certainly ate lentils in ancient Rome, where their Latin name was *lenticula*, and in medieval France, where they were known as *lentilles*. Although the green *lentilles du Puy* may be the gourmet's choice, green lentils are also produced in Umbria in southern Italy, where this soup still makes a substantial and popular meal.

Method Put the lentils, onions, garlic, fennel, carrots, tomatoes, tomato paste, rosemary, thyme, and bay leaves into a large pot. Pour in 6 cups of water. Bring to a boil and simmer until the lentils are starting to become tender—about 15-20 minutes.

While they're cooking, season the meat with salt and pepper, and roll into balls about the size of walnuts. Heat the oil in a large pan and fry the meat-balls until they're brown all over. Remove the bay leaves and the woody stems of the rosemary and thyme from the lentil mixture.

Add the meatballs to the lentils and simmer until both lentils and meatballs are cooked—about 25 minutes. Serve sprinkled with the chopped parsley on top.

Chicken with matzo dumplings (knaidlach)

Serves 4-6

For the broth

You can use good-quality, low-salt kosher chicken stock cubes or bouillon powder, but this home-made broth is infinitely better.

1 leftover chicken carcass, all skin and fat removed

2 Spanish onions, 1 whole and unpeeled, the other peeled and chopped

1 leek, coarsely chopped

3 celery stalks, with leaves if possible, coarsely chopped

4 bay leaves

1 large sprig of rosemary

2 large sprigs of thyme

1 large sprig of sage

4 large sprigs of parsley

12 white peppercorns

For the dumplings (knaidlach)

7 ounces medium matzo meal (about 8 matzo sheets, ground up)

3 eggs

1 tablespoon olive oil

1 tablespoon finely chopped flat-leaf parsley

3 grindings of black pepper

2 pinches of salt

This recipe makes a clear broth, but if you wish to turn it into a concentrated chicken broth, continue simmering until the volume is reduced by half. It can then be strained and frozen and used in many of the other recipes in this book. Of course, you can remove the carcass and the unpeeled onion, return any remaining chicken meat to the pot and serve as a more substantial chicken and vegetable soup, omitting the dumplings (knaidlach).

If you don't have a chicken carcass, boil a whole chicken for the soup and use the meat in other dishes, such as Greek chicken patties (see page 42). Traditionally, a boiling fowl from a kosher butcher would be used.

Method First, make the broth. Put the carcass in a large pot and cover with about 2½ quarts (10 cups) water. Bring to a boil, cover, and simmer for 30 minutes. Add the vegetables, herbs, and peppercorns, return to a boil, cover and simmer for 1 hour. Strain, reserving the broth.

Make the dumplings by mixing all the dumpling ingredients together, then knead until you have a smooth dough, adding a little water if necessary. Cover and let rest for at least 3 hours.

Using your hands, form the mixture into balls the size of apricots.

To put it all together, bring the chicken broth up to simmering point. Drop in the dumplings and continue simmering, covered, for 30 minutes.

Health note This is the famous "Jewish penicillin" beloved of every mother and grandmother. It's not an old wives' tale; there's good scientific evidence that it contains vitamins, minerals, and other natural chemicals that are antibacterial and immune-boosting. In addition, nutrients and valuable plant chemicals are extracted from the vegetables and herbs during the cooking process, most of which end up as active ingredients in the finished soup.

Glass flask   This beautifully proportioned 19th-century flask was used on the Sabbath for oil, or more probably wine, and is engraved with verses from the Bible that formed part of the Kiddush blessing. The inscription on the neck is a decorative Arabic script that is apparently meaningless. It is thought that the bottle was made in Syria by Mordecai Shiqfaati, but its round base means that it cannot stand up unsupported—not the most practical design for a household object.

vegetables and salads

Red cabbage with apples and caraway

Serves 4

1 medium red cabbage, finely
*   shredded*
1 tablespoon cider vinegar
1 teaspoon caraway seeds
2 tablespoons raw sugar (if
*   unavailable, use light*
*   brown sugar)*
2 large cooking apples, peeled,
*   cored, and quartered*

Cabbage was one of the few vegetables available to Ashkenazi Jews in the harsh climate of Eastern Europe. In Western Europe, although a large range of produce was readily available, cabbage remained a firm favorite.

Caraway is native to India, Asia, and parts of southern Europe, and gets its name from the Arabic *al-karawiya* ("the cumin"), which was used as medicine by the ancient Egyptians. In fact, fossilized seeds have been excavated from sites 5,000 years old, and they have also been found where caravans followed the Silk Route. By the time Shakespeare mentioned caraway in *Henry IV*, it was already a popular flavoring in Germany and England. This typically German recipe uses the seed not only to flavor the cabbage, but also to reduce the dish's "flatulence factor."

Delicious hot or cold, this dish goes well with cold meat, fish, and other salads.

Method Put the cabbage, vinegar, caraway seeds, and sugar into a large pot. Add a ½ cup of water and bring to a boil. Put the apples on top, cover the pot and simmer gently until the cabbage is tender and the apples are mushy—about 40 minutes.

Remove carefully to a serving dish, trying to leave most of the apples on top of the cabbage.

Health note Long regarded as "the medicine of the poor," all cabbage provides exceptional health benefits: protection from cancer, improved digestive function, an abundance of vitamin C and folic acid, and, in the red cabbage used here, substantial quantities of beta carotene.

Spiced leeks

Serves 4

About 2 cups vegetable
broth–see recipe for Barley with
mushrooms and marjoram
(page 47) or use a good-quality,
low-salt cube or bouillon powder
2 bay leaves, broken in half
across the spines
1 teaspoon coriander seeds
1 teaspoon caraway seeds
8 small leeks, cleaned and trimmed
but left whole
1/4 cup olive oil

Leeks grew wild in biblical times and were very popular with the ancient Hebrews. They've remained so ever since in both Sephardic and Ashkenazi communities. Because cultivated leeks thrive in cold climates as well as they do in the Mediterranean (in fact, they taste much better after a touch of frost), they were a common addition to soups, stews, and roast meats.

Served here as a vegetable in their own right, they have all the cardio-protective benefits of their relatives, onions and garlic, and also help in the relief of coughs and colds. In ancient Rome, they were specially cultivated on the orders of Nero, who ate leeks every day to improve his voice. I don't know if it was wandering Jews who introduced them to the Welsh, but it's possible…

Method Bring the broth to a boil. Add the bay leaves, coriander and caraway seeds, and boil briskly for 1 minute.

Put the leeks into a heavy pan and pour in the broth and olive oil. Cover and simmer (on the stove) until the leeks are tender–about 25 minutes. Put the leeks onto a serving dish and keep warm.

Remove the bay leaves and reduce the cooking liquid by boiling briskly, uncovered, for about 5 minutes. Pour the liquid over the leeks to serve.

Sweet and sour zucchini

Serves 4

1/4 cup olive oil
8 large zucchinis, cut into
large cubes
1 tablespoon finely chopped
fresh oregano leaves
1 small garlic clove, finely chopped
3 tablespoons red wine vinegar
3 tablespoons raw sugar (if
unavailable, use light
brown sugar)
1/2 teaspoon ground cinnamon

Sicilian Jews adopted this Turkish recipe that combines the exotic but typical sweet-and-sour tastes of sugar, vinegar, and cinnamon. It's yet another example of how tasty zucchini can be when treated with a little imagination.

Method Warm the oil in a large frying pan and sauté the zucchini, stirring frequently, until softened but not brown.

Using a slotted spoon, put onto a serving plate and sprinkle with the oregano. Add the garlic, vinegar, sugar, cinnamon, and about 2 tablespoons water to the oil remaining in the pan. Bring to a boil and simmer until thickened. Serve the zucchini with the sauce poured on top.

Health note Here we have heart protection from the garlic, beta carotene from the zucchini, and antibacterial phytochemicals from the cinnamon.

Fava beans in olive oil

Serves 4

*About 4 1/2 pounds fava beans
    (unshelled weight) or about
    5–5 1/2 cups shelled*
*About 2 cups vegetable
    broth—see recipe for Barley
    with mushrooms and marjoram
    (page 47) or use a good-quality,
    low-salt cube or bouillon powder*
1 large sprig of rosemary
*2 tablespoons finely chopped
    flat-leaf parsley*
1/2 cup extra-virgin olive oil
Black pepper

Fava beans have remained popular in all Jewish communities and they're frequently eaten during Passover as a reminder of Jewish slavery in Egypt, where they formed part of the staple diet. Many fava bean dishes are found in the Sephardic cooking of Greece, Italy, and southern France as well as in all Middle Eastern Jewish cuisines.

Also known as broad beans, they are an old Eurasian member of the legume family, and are delicious raw when they're young.

Serve warm or cold, as a vegetable dish or salad.

Method Put the beans into a saucepan and just cover with broth. Add the rosemary, bring to a boil, and cook over high heat, uncovered, until the beans are cooked (about 7 minutes), adding more broth or water if necessary. Remove the rosemary.

Mix the parsley with the olive oil and stir into the beans. Serve sprinkled with freshly ground black pepper.

Health note Fava beans contain minerals such as iron, zinc, phosphorus, and manganese and are also a source of folic acid and vitamin E. They're low in fat, rich in beta carotene, and supply the valuable soluble fiber which helps lower cholesterol levels. They provide good levels of protein and, when eaten together with starchy foods like rice or pasta, they're as good as steak.

Turnips and carrots with garlic

Serves 4

12 garlic cloves, peeled but
   left whole

8 baby turnips, scrubbed, or
   2 older turnips, peeled and cubed

8 baby carrots, scrubbed, or
   3 older carrots, peeled and cut up

6 tablespoons olive oil

1 sprig of chervil

1 tablespoon honey

2 tablespoons finely chopped
   flat-leaf parsley,

Carrots are another favorite in traditional Jewish cooking. Like potatoes and cabbage, they were among the few vegetables which survived the harsh climate of Eastern Europe, and were cooked as the traditional dish *tzimmes*: glazed with sugar or honey and always eaten during Rosh Hashanah. Like other sweet dishes eaten during the New Year celebrations, they symbolized a wish that the coming year would be sweet.

Although turnips were popular in parts of the Sephardic world, especially in Iraq, Egypt, and Lebanon, where they were mostly eaten as pickles or sweetmeats, they were more widely used by European Jews in stews and with roast meats. They have a wonderful ability to absorb juices and flavors, which is why they make such a good accompaniment to fatty dishes like duck and goose. Turnips were particularly popular with Dutch Jews—which is where this recipes originates.

Method Put the garlic into a large pot of cold water, bring to a boil and boil for 5 minutes. Drain and set aside.

Put the turnips and carrots into a large pot with half the olive oil, the chervil, honey, and just enough water to cover. Simmer, covered, until just tender: about 10-15 minutes. Remove the lid, turn the heat to high, and boil off the cooking liquid.

Put the garlic into a very large frying pan and sauté gently in the remaining olive oil. Add the garlic and juices to the turnips and carrots and mix well. Sprinkle with the parsley for serving.

Pomegranate with avocado salad

Serves 4

1 pomegranate

3 ounces (about ½ cup) seedless
   black grapes, cut in half

2 ripe avocados

Special vinaigrette (see page 82)

2 tablespoons freshly chopped
   mint leaves

Pomegranates have great significance in Jewish cooking. They originated in Asia, where they grow as a shrub or small tree, and have long been cultivated for their edible fruit, with their tough red outer rind, many seeds, and luscious red pulp. They get their name from the Latin words *pomum* and *granatum*, meaning "apple" and "full of seeds."

As children, my cousins and I always looked forward to the festival of Rosh Hashanah, the Jewish New Year: a time when all Jews pray for a year of health, peace, and prosperity. All children like sweet things, and this is the time when bread is dipped in honey, followed by slices of apple dipped in honey and the blessing: "May it be Your will to renew for us a good and sweet year." It was also the tradition to eat pomegranates, which we did by cutting them in half and picking out the flesh-colored seeds with a pin. The significance is that our good deeds will be increased like the seeds of the pomegranate. The seeds also signify the desire for many children to be born in the coming year.

Method Cut the pomegranate in half and use a teaspoon to remove the seeds. Combine with the grapes.

Immediately before serving, cut the avocado in half, peel it, remove the pit and cut into slices. (If you leave avocado pieces sitting on the side, they'll discolor.) Mix together gently with the pomegranates and grapes. Dress with the vinaigrette. Scatter with the mint leaves for serving.

Health note This exotic fruit is full of health-enhancing carotenoids, vitamins, and fiber. Avocados are one of the most nutritious of all vegetables (see page 56) and, despite what many people think, they're not fattening.

Olive and orange salad

Serves 4

4 oranges, peeled and sliced
horizontally

About 18 black olives, pitted and
cut in half

Juice of 1 lemon

1/4 cup extra-virgin olive oil

1 garlic clove, very finely chopped

1 teaspoon finely chopped fresh
mint

1/2 teaspoon ground cumin

1/2 teaspoon paprika, plus
2 pinches for serving

Jews were the earliest cultivators of citrus fruits. Olives have been cultivated for at least 5,000 years, and they're part of Jewish biblical history. Widely used in Sephardic cuisine, this salad is a favorite in Israel, although its origins are probably north African.

Don't remove all the pith from the oranges as it contains bioflavonoids that protect the walls of blood vessels.

Method Put the oranges into a serving bowl. Scatter the olives over the oranges.

Whisk together the lemon juice, olive oil, garlic, mint, cumin, and paprika. Pour the dressing over the salad, adding 2 pinches of paprika for serving.

Health note This recipe combines the taste and vitamin C of oranges with the bitter flavors of olives. Because they're such a good source of oil, olives are often thought to be fattening, but this isn't the case; 18 olives contain only 60 calories, but they provide some vitamin E and lots of protective antioxidants.

Green beans with onion and thyme

Serves 4

1 medium onion or red onion,
   finely sliced

3 tablespoons olive oil

1 1/4 pounds green beans, topped
   and tailed (frozen will do
   if you can't find fresh)

2 large sprigs of thyme

1/2 handful of chives,
   finely chopped

Thyme grows wild throughout the southern Mediterranean and was a popular herb with Jewish cooks, whose historical use of culinary herbs can be traced back to the Old Testament. As well as its unmistakable flavor, thyme has many medicinal properties. It was used by the ancient Egyptians for embalming, Greeks burned it in their temples, and Romans used its antiseptic properties for cleaning their houses.

This recipe comes from a tiny Jewish (but not kosher) restaurant in Nice and is equally delicious cold as part of a salad meal or buffet.

Method Put the onion into a large saucepan and sauté gently in the oil until soft but not brown. Add the beans, thyme, and about 1 cup of water—just enough to cover the beans.

Cover the pan and cook over medium heat until the beans are just tender—about 10 minutes. Remove the thyme. Drain the beans and sprinkle with the chives for serving.

Health note Thyme is a powerful antiseptic and you've probably seen the essential oil thymol extracted from this plant in the pink mouthwash by your dentist's chair.

Beans in garlic

Serves 4-6

2 tablespoons olive oil

2 garlic cloves, finely chopped

3 scallions, diagonally sliced

2 tablespoons tomato paste

18 ounces green beans, topped,
   tailed, and cut into 1-inch pieces

1 tablespoon chopped fresh
   oregano leaves

In some parts of the world, Jews are known as "the garlic-and onion-eaters." Wandering in the wilderness, Jews remembered the garlic and onions they'd eaten in Egypt (as mentioned in the Book of Numbers, Chapter 11). In fact, the whole allium genus, which also includes shallots, scallions (green onions), chives, and leeks, has valuable healing powers.

Method Heat the oil and gently sauté the garlic and scallions for 3 minutes. Add the tomato paste and mix well. Add the beans and just enough water to cover. Stir in the oregano. Cover and simmer until the beans are just tender—about 10 minutes.

Remove the lid and turn the heat to high to reduce the cooking juices—no longer than 2 minutes.

Serve the beans in the juices.

Health note This recipe provides heart-protective, cholesterol-lowering, anticoagulant and blood-pressure-reducing chemicals in abundance. As a bonus, garlic and onions are also helpful for many types of infection, especially coughs and colds. The beans add fiber and beta carotene.

Opposite: *Green beans with onion and thyme*

Orange beets with almonds

Serves 4

4 medium cooked beets
(NOT pickled), cubed

2 ¼ cups freshly squeezed
orange juice

Orange zest (optional)

5 tablespoons olive oil

3 ounces (about ³/₄ cup) sliced
almonds

The ancient Greeks used beets as a medicine and also as offerings to their gods. In Eastern Europe, this vibrant red vegetable is valued as a blood strengthener. It is found throughout Europe, North Africa, and Asia, and especially in Poland and Russia, where beets soup is a national dish.

This recipe combines two favorite Jewish ingredients: beets, which have been part of Jewish cuisine since around the 4th century, and almonds, which are mentioned in the Book of Genesis. In both Ashkenazi and Sephardic communities, almonds are a symbolic food on all festive occasions. They are rich in protein, vital minerals, and B vitamins, and make a perfect companion to the valuable nutrients present in beets.

Method Put the beets, orange juice, orange zest, if using, and olive oil in a pan and simmer gently for about 10 minutes. Turn up the heat and boil until most of the liquid is reduced.

Meanwhile, dry-fry the almonds until just golden—about 2 minutes. Serve the beets in their juice with the almonds scattered on top.

Fava beans with beets

Serves 4

8 ounces (about 1 1/2–1 3/4 cups)
   fava beans

4 medium cooked beets, cubed

About 2 tablespoons extra-virgin
   olive oil

Black pepper

**For the magic mayonnaise
(optional)**

6 tablespoons of mayonnaise
   (homemade, of course, is best)
   and add one of the following:

1 tablespoon capers, rinsed,
   squeezed dry, and chopped

2 gherkins, chopped

2 tablespoons chopped "soft"
   herbs: chervil, marjoram, basil,
   oregano, etc., not woody herbs
   like rosemary

1 teaspoon Dijon mustard

A few chopped scallions or anything
   else that takes your fancy

This is another of my mother's favorite recipes. It combines the beet traditions of her own Ashkenazi background with the Sephardic love of fava beans and the Dutch passion for mayonnaise. The beans with mayonnaise came from her Dutch mother-in-law, and she added the beets.

A note to orthodox Jews: be wary because some milk by-products may be used in both commercially prepared mayonnaise and ready-made mustard. This is important if you're eating the dish with a meat meal.

Method Cook the fava beans in boiling water until almost tender. Add the beets and continue cooking for another 5 minutes. Drain, drizzle with olive oil, and serve hot with a few twists of freshly ground black pepper.

Alternatively, serve cold accompanied by the mayonnaise.

Health note Beans and beets are exceptionally healthy: good for the blood, circulation, heart, and natural resistance. Mayonnaise does, of course, contain some cholesterol, but unless you already have exceptionally high cholesterol levels, it's the cholesterol your body manufactures from saturated animal fat that does the damage—so don't worry about the eggs in the mayonnaise.

Warm onion salad with cucumber and capers

Serves 4

For the special vinaigrette
1/2 cup extra-virgin olive oil
2 tablespoons walnut oil
2 tablespoons cider vinegar
1/2 teaspoon mustard powder
1/2 teaspoon brown sugar

For the salad
2 medium onions, unpeeled
2 tablespoons capers
8-inch cucumber, peeled, seeded,
  and chopped

Onions have been part of Jewish cuisine since ancient Egyptian times; there are biblical references to this delicious and healthy vegetable.

You may think that roasting vegetables is an invention of modern trendy chefs, but Jews have been doing it for centuries. This method of cooking imparts a unique flavor which, thanks to the vegetables' natural sugars and the small amount of added sugar, is enhanced by gentle caramelization. To enjoy it at its best, this salad should be eaten warm—not hot or cold.

Method First, make the vinaigrette by putting all the ingredients into a bowl and whisking thoroughly—or put them into a screw-top jar and shake vigorously.

To make the salad, preheat the oven to 350°F. Put the onions in a baking dish and roast for about 1 hour, or until they feel soft. Peel off the outer skins and cut the white flesh into quarters.

Rinse the capers in running water, then squash them gently with your fingertips. Put the onions and cucumber into a serving dish, scatter the capers over them, and sprinkle with the Special vinaigrette.

Roast tomatoes with garlic

Serves 4

4 large tomatoes, cut in half

*2 tablespoons fresh whole-wheat
bread crumbs*

1 garlic clove, very finely chopped

6 large basil leaves, coarsely torn

Tomatoes came to Europe from South America with the Spanish explorers, and the Sephardic Jews took them back to North America and to the Middle East when the Inquisition forced them out of Spain.

The sharp taste of garlic and the wonderful aroma of basil have made this a popular dish which can be served hot as a vegetable or cold as an appetizer or part of a buffet. Simple to make, it is a rich source of the protective antioxidant lycopene, in the tomatoes, and the cholesterol-lowering benefits of garlic.

Method Preheat the oven to 350°F. Put the tomatoes into a shallow baking tray, cut side up.

Mix together the bread crumbs, garlic, and basil. Push the bread crumb mixture gently into the tomato halves. Bake for 20 minutes.

Braised carrots

Serves 4

3 tablespoons olive oil

*8 young carrots, with the bottom
¹/₂-inch of their leaves*

*About 1 cup vegetable
broth—see recipe for Barley
with mushrooms and marjoram
(page 47) or use a good-quality,
low-salt cube or bouillon powder*

1 tablespoon finely chopped mint

¹/₄ cup raisins

*2 tablespoons finely chopped
flat-leaf parsley*

Carrots are widely used in all Jewish communities, from the coldest parts of Eastern Europe to the kitchens of the Mediterranean and the hot-spots of the Middle East, Asia, and India. Adding mint and raisins is typical of Middle Eastern and north African Jewish and Muslim cooking.

Method Heat the olive oil in a large frying pan and sauté the carrots gently until golden all over—about 6 minutes. Add enough broth (or water) just to cover. Add the mint and raisins. Cover and simmer until the carrots are almost tender—about 15 minutes.

Uncover and bring to a brisk boil until most of the liquid has evaporated. Sprinkle with the parsley for serving.

Health note Rich in cancer-fighting beta carotene, carrots are one of the few vegetables that are better eaten cooked than raw, as the cooking process makes the nutrients easier for your body to extract. The oil in this recipe improves absorption of beta carotene, a fat-soluble nutrient that is also good for night vision.

Zucchini salad

Serves 4

8 baby zucchinis
Juice of 1/2 lemon
3 tablespoons extra-virgin olive oil
1/2 teaspoon ground allspice

Most squashes have little flavor but, like sponges, they soak up the tastes of herbs and spices—which is why they are paired here with allspice. Popular throughout the Ottoman Empire, allspice isn't, as many people think, a mixture of lots of spices; it's the whole or powdered seeds of a tropical tree called *Pimenta officinalis* with an intriguing flavor that tastes like a mixture of nutmeg, cloves, and cinnamon. Sometimes referred to as Jamaica pepper, it's widely used in Turkey and north Africa.

Method Simmer the zucchinis in salted water until soft. Drain and squeeze gently (use a fine mesh strainer or cheesecloth). Chop coarsely.

  Mix together the lemon juice, oil, and allspice. Pour them over the zucchini and serve cold.

Health note There is no need to peel these baby vegetables, which means you get fiber and beta carotene from this recipe as well as vitamin C from the lemon juice and digestive benefits from the allspice.

Celery braised in walnut oil

Serves 4

2 celery hearts, cut in half
*   lengthwise (save the leaves)*
1/4 cup tablespoons walnut oil
3 tablespoons lemon juice
1 teaspoon brown sugar
1 teaspoon chopped fresh sage

Celery has always been a popular vegetable. Widely used in stews and with roast meats in western European and North American Ashkenazi cooking, it is also favored by Sephardi cooks for its unique flavor. Here, simply braised over low heat to preserve its nutrients, it has a surprisingly delicate and interesting taste.

Method Put all of the ingredients, including the celery leaves, together in a pan wide enough to hold the celery in a single layer.

  Turn the celery hearts over gently so that they're covered with the liquid ingredients. Cover and simmer gently for about 35 minutes.

Health note One stalk of celery contains only 7 calories, and you really do use more to chew and digest it than it provides. Although very poor in conventional nutrients, celery has great medicinal value as a gentle diuretic. Ensure you eat the leaves for their beta carotene and folic acid.

Lettuce with anchovies

Serves 4

4 Bibb lettuces, cut in half lengthwise

1 tablespoon fennel seeds

2/3 cup olive oil

About 1 1/4 cups vegetable broth—see recipe for Barley with mushrooms and marjoram (page 47) or use a good-quality, low-salt cube or bouillon powder

8 canned anchovy fillets, preferably in olive oil

The ancient Greek physicians knew that wild lettuce was a great cure for insomnia. They used to extract the sticky sap from the stalks and concentrate it to make a potent sleeping potion. All modern lettuces are descended from the same family and, although they're not so potent, they are still calming, relaxing, and mildly soporific.

The ancient Romans loved to combine the harsh taste of salted anchovies with the slight bitterness of lettuce. Whether this preference was taken to Rome by the Jews or acquired from the Romans by the Jews who settled there isn't known. It's certain, however, that both ingredients appeal to Jewish palates, and you'll find variations on this recipe in the Jewish communities of Spain, Portugal, southern France, Greece, and Italy.

Method Preheat the oven to 350°F. Put the lettuce halves into a casserole dish. Scatter with the fennel seeds and pour the oil over them.

Heat the broth and pour it over the lettuces, ensuring that they're just covered; top up with boiling water if necessary. Cover with foil and bake for 25 minutes.

Remove from the oven, arrange the anchovy fillets over the lettuces, and return to the oven, covered with foil, for 10 minutes.

Nutty spinach with raisins

Serves 4

2 ounces (about 1/3 cup)
seedless raisins
1/4 cup pine nuts
2 tablespoons olive oil
1 garlic clove, very finely sliced
2 1/4 pounds baby spinach
Juice of 1/2 lemon

The combination of spinach, nuts, and dried fruits is a common favorite with Jews and Muslims in the Middle East and north Africa. This recipe comes from Rome, but it was almost certainly taken there by Jewish traders during the days of the Roman Empire. It has now migrated into the general realm of Italian cooking and is normally eaten warm rather than hot.

Delicious served cold as a salad, but if you're having a non-meat meal, you could crumble feta cheese as well as (or instead of) the lemon juice on top and still be kosher.

Method Soak the raisins in freshly boiled water for 10 minutes, and dry-roast the pine nuts.

Put the olive oil into a large pot and sauté the garlic very gently for 2 minutes. Wash the spinach, even if the packaging says it's ready-washed, and add to the garlic pot with only the water clinging to the leaves. Cook, covered, over gentle heat until the spinach is wilted—not more than 5 minutes.

Drain the raisins and add to the spinach along with the toasted pine nuts, stirring them in gently. Serve with the lemon juice squeezed on top.

Health note With all the nutrients in spinach (especially the beta carotene), protein and minerals from the pine nuts, and heart-protective properties from garlic, this is exceptionally healthy. Adding feta cheese provides a bonus of extra calcium.

Boulangère potatoes

Serves 4

About 2 tablespoons olive oil

3 medium onions, finely sliced

1 1/2 pounds Russet or yellow
*   potatoes, peeled and thinly sliced*

2 bay leaves, torn in half

1 garlic clove, finely chopped

2 tablespoons thyme leaves

3 cups chicken broth—see recipe
*   for Chicken soup with matzo*
*   dumplings (page 66), or*
*   use a good-quality, low-salt*
*   stock cube or bouillon powder*

Black pepper

Potatoes are one of the vegetable mainstays of Ashkenazi cooking from Eastern Europe, where they were one of the few abundant vegetables. This recipe also has the more Mediterranean influences of garlic, thyme, and bay leaves.

I haven't been able to find the origins of the title, but this is a popular French/Jewish recipe and I can only guess that it was taken in its pot to the village *boulanger* (baker)—possibly before the start of Sabbath—hence the name *boulangère* (baker's wife). However it came to be named, it is extremely healthy.

Method Preheat the oven to 425°F. Brush a little of the olive oil around a large flameproof casserole dish or other heavy ovenproof pan.

Gently sauté the onions in the remaining oil until soft but not brown. Put the onions in the bottom of the casserole dish. Arrange the potato slices in layers on top, with the bay leaves, garlic, and thyme leaves distributed equally.

Pour the broth over them and scatter a few generous grindings of black pepper on top. Bake for 35 minutes, occasionally pushing the potatoes gently into the broth if necessary.

Eggplant rice

Serves 4

1 large eggplant, peeled and cubed

About 2 teaspoons sea salt or
kosher salt

3 tablespoons olive oil

1 medium onion, finely sliced

1 garlic clove, finely sliced

14 ounces (about 2 cups) long-grain
white rice

4 cups vegetable broth—
see recipe for Barley with
mushrooms and marjoram
(page 47) or use a good-quality,
low-salt stock cube or bouillon
powder

The wonderful eggplant has a truly ancient history; it has certainly been known in India for at least 3,000 years and was used in China several hundred years before the Common Era. Together with rice, it was introduced to Italy by the Arabs in the 10th century, but was already popular with Middle Eastern and Sephardic Jews.

This dish is a Sicilian version of risotto. As well as being a super-healthy side dish, it also makes a good appetizer or light meal—and you can serve it hot or cold.

Method Put the eggplants into a colander, sprinkle with salt, leave for 30 minutes, rinse thoroughly, and wipe dry.

Warm the oil in a large, wide pan and sauté the onion and garlic until soft but not browned. Add the rice and stir until all the grains are covered with oil. Add the eggplant cubes and stir until covered with the oil. Start adding the broth, a ladleful at a time, and keep stirring until each ladleful is absorbed. Continue until you've used up all the broth and the rice is tender and nearly dry. Serve hot or cold. If serving it cold, you may have to stir in an extra tablespoon or so of olive oil.

Ceramic plate   This is a piece of Lambeth pottery, c. 1720. The script in the center of the plate is the Hebrew word for meat and there is a similar plate for milk in the Museum of London. The Delft blue-and-white coloring is unusual on such a plate because the conventional coloring was red for meat and blue or green for dairy. It is probable that the plate was so labeled to help the servants keep the milk and meat utensils separate—this clearly belonged to an orthodox family.

main courses

Vegetarian cholent

Serves 4-6

2 tablespoons olive oil

1 onion, finely chopped

2 garlic cloves, finely chopped

8 ounces (about 1 ½ cups)
   whole-grain barley

6 ounces (about 1 cup) canned
   butter beans (drained weight)
   –if unavailable, use limas

2 tablespoons chopped flat-leaf
   parsley

2 tablespoons flour, seasoned with
   4 grindings of black pepper

About 12 ounces Russet or yellow
   potatoes, unpeeled but thinly
   sliced, about 2 ⅓ to 2 ⅔ cups

About 4 cups vegetable broth–
   see recipe for Barley with
   mushrooms and marjoram
   (page 47) or use a good-quality,
   low-salt stock cube or bouillon
   powder

For observant Jews throughout the world, it's forbidden to light a fire, turn on an oven, or strike a match between the hours of sunset on Friday and sunset on Saturday. For this reason, the slow-cooked casserole is a common factor for Ashkenazi, Sephardi, Indian, Greek, Russian, Polish, and British Jews. Whatever their culinary heritage, the principles remain the same. In the villages of Eastern Europe, people took their own pot to the baker, where it went into the ovens when the last bread came out on Friday afternoon. At the end of the Sabbath, the pots were collected and taken home for the evening meal. The most common dish was *cholent*, and most housewives kept a pot that was used for nothing else. The British and American versions owe their origins to Eastern Europe, where cholent was eaten to keep out the bitter cold of winter. Just the thought of this massive pot of fatty meat, beans, marrow bones, dumplings, potatoes, and even chicken fat is enough to cause a heart attack—sorry, but this is the very worst of Jewish cooking.

According to Claudia Roden, in her wonderful *Book of Jewish Food*, cholent is an ancient descendant of the French cassoulet and gets its name from the medieval French *chaud* (hot) and *lent* (slow). The version here is much closer to that eaten by poor Jews who couldn't afford meat; *cholent* became lethal only with affluence. Serve with steamed broccoli florets mixed with crushed blanched almonds.

Method Preheat the oven to 350°F. Heat the oil in a large flameproof casserole dish or other heavy ovenproof pan and gently sauté the onion and garlic until softened but not brown. Add the barley, beans, and parsley.

Sprinkle the seasoned flour in the contents. Layer the potatoes on top and pour in the stock. Cover with a lid or aluminum foil and cook for 50 minutes.

Health note This recipe won't give you a heart attack and it will actually help to lower cholesterol, reduce blood pressure, and protect your heart and circulatory system.

Lentil rissoles with crushed tomato sauce

Serves 4-6

For the rissoles

6 ounces (about 1 cup) lentils

About ¼ cup canola (rapeseed)
  or sunflower oil

1 medium onion, finely chopped

1 garlic clove, finely chopped

1 large carrot, grated

1 tablespoon finely chopped
  flat-leaf parsley

1 teaspoon finely chopped
  fresh cilantro

1 teaspoon ground cumin

1 large egg, beaten

3 tablespoons fresh whole-wheat
  bread crumbs

6 tablespoons coarse matzo meal

About 4 tablespoons olive oil,
  for frying

For the crushed tomato sauce

5 medium tomatoes

Dash of Tabasco sauce

1 teaspoon raw sugar or light
  brown, if unavailable

⅔ cup olive oil

6 basil leaves

From southern Europe to the Middle East and India, lentils have been a staple food for centuries. Lentil rissoles may sound like a music-hall-joke vegetarian recipe, but properly handled they're versatile, extremely nutritious, and they taste great, too.

Serve with Warm onion salad with cucumbers and capers (see page 82) and fresh garden peas. These rissoles can also be served cold if you leave out the Crushed tomato sauce and serve them with a Pomegranate with avocado salad (see page 75) or even a tomato and scallion salad with Special vinaigrette (see page 82).

Method First, make the rissoles. Wash the lentils thoroughly and simmer in boiling water according to the package instructions—usually about 20-25 minutes, but some lentils need soaking, then cooking for up to 1 hour. Drain well.

While they're cooking, heat the oil in a large pan and gently sauté the onion and garlic until soft but not brown. Add the carrot and continue cooking gently for 5 more minutes. Stir in the lentils, herbs, and cumin, and heat gently for another 5 minutes. Pour into a large heatproof bowl, add the egg and bread crumbs, and combine thoroughly until the mixture holds its shape, adding more bread crumbs if necessary.

Using your hands, form into 4-6 rissoles. Put the matzo meal onto a dinner plate and dip each rissole into it, covering all over. Put about 4 tablespoons olive oil into a frying pan and fry the rissoles, in batches if necessary, for about 5 minutes each side, until golden, adding more oil as needed.

Put all the ingredients for the sauce into a blender or food processor and whizz until well combined. Warm through, and pour the sauce over the rissoles for serving.

Health note Lentils contains protein, B vitamins, iron, zinc, and calcium. Combined with carrots and fresh herbs, for beta carotene and good digestion, these rissoles have the added bonus of huge amounts of protective lycopene from the crushed tomato sauce.

Mediterranean medley

Serves 4

2 garlic cloves, finely chopped

1 onion, finely chopped

1/4 cup olive oil

1 teaspoon chopped fresh oregano

4 tomatoes, finely sliced

9 ounces buffalo mozzarella,
  sliced to the same size as
  the tomatoes

8 zucchinis, sliced to the same
  size as the tomatoes and
  mozzarella

1/4 cup grated Parmesan cheese

6 dill fronds

I was eleven years old when my father took us on vacation to France. After a week driving through the war-ravaged areas of the north of the country, we finally ended up in Nice, where for the first time I tasted the wonders of Mediterranean cooking.

One evening we ate with a Jewish family my father had known before the war. In 1950, it was almost impossible to get kosher meat in that part of the world, so we ate this wonderful vegetarian dish. I'd never seen zucchini or mozzarella cheese and never tasted olive oil. Protein, calcium, vitamins, and flavor abound in this simple dish—and it's just as good hot or cold. Serve with baby new potatoes boiled in their skins.

Method Preheat the oven to 350°F. Sauté the garlic and onion gently in the olive oil until soft but not browned. Mix with the oregano and put them in the bottom of a large, shallow casserole dish. Arrange the tomatoes, mozzarella, and zucchini alternately in layers on top. Cover with aluminum foil and bake for about an hour, or until the juices start running.

Sprinkle with the Parmesan, turn up the oven to 400°F, and bake for another 15 minutes. Serve with the dill fronds on top.

Spiced vegetable lasagne

Serves 6

For the white sauce
1/4 cup (1/2 stick) unsalted butter
3 tablespoons flour
1/2 teaspoon ground cumin
2 1/4 cups soy milk

For the lasagne
1 large onion, finely chopped
1 garlic clove, finely chopped
About 3 tablespoons olive oil
3 zucchinis, cubed
1 large eggplant, cubed
3 large, thin-skinned tomatoes,
  coarsely chopped
1 tablespoon tomato paste
3 tablespoons finely chopped fresh
  oregano (or 1 tablespoon dried)
14 ounces dried lasagne,
  cooked according to the
  package instructions
3 tablespoons grated Parmesan
  cheese
6 dill fronds

Italy is one of the better countries for vegetarian travelers. Although there are few native vegetarians, so much of their wonderful Mediterranean culinary repertoire is based on non-meat dishes that there is inevitably a reasonable vegetarian choice in most cafés and restaurants. This Italian Jewish favorite became widely popular as a result of the massive increase in tourism during the 1960s and 70s.

Serve with a large bowl of mixed greens and scallion salad with Special vinaigrette (see page 82).

Method First, make the white sauce. Melt the butter gently in a large frying pan. Remove from the heat and stir in the flour and cumin. Return to a gentle heat and cook, stirring continuously, for 2 minutes. Gradually add the soy milk, still stirring continuously, until thickened.

To make the lasagne, preheat the oven to 425°F. In a large pan sweat the onion and garlic gently in 2 tablespoons of the oil until softened but not browned. Add the zucchini, eggplant, tomatoes, tomato paste and oregano, and continue cooking for 5 minutes, stirring continuously.

Grease a wide, shallow, ovenproof pasta dish with the olive oil. Put in one layer of the cooked lasagne sheets. Add half the vegetable mixture and a third of the white sauce. Add another layer of the lasagne sheets. Follow with the remaining vegetable mixture and another third of the sauce. Add another layer of lasagne sheets and the remaining sauce, making sure the pasta is well covered with the sauce.

Bake for 15 minutes. Remove from the oven, sprinkle with the Parmesan and dill, and return to the oven for 5 minutes.

Health note Healthy enough on its own, with all the protective benefits of onions, garlic, and the vegetables, the white sauce is made here with soy milk for extra isoflavones. These hormone-like chemicals help protect against osteoporosis and menstrual problems.

Fish with prunes and tomatoes

Serves 4

4 cod steaks

8 ready-to-eat pitted prunes,
  cut in half

8 cherry tomatoes, cut in half

1/4 cup olive oil

2/3 cup dry white wine

4 large dill fronds

Black pepper

The combination of dried fruits with meat, poultry, and fish was popular from the earliest times throughout the Middle East, north Africa, and the Mediterranean, including Greece. In this incredibly healthy recipe from Thessalonika, the only fat comes from the heart-protective monounsaturated fat in the olive oil.

Delicious served with noodles or fried rice and Celery braised in walnut oil (see page 86).

Method Preheat the oven to 350°F. Put the fish in one layer in a large casserole dish, or baking pan. Arrange the prunes and tomatoes around the fish. Pour the olive oil and white wine over them, then add the dill fronds and 3 grindings of black pepper.

Cover with a lid or aluminum foil and bake for 30 minutes.

Health note The fish provides protein, vitamins, and minerals, especially iodine, which is essential for proper functioning of the thyroid gland and is frequently deficient in the average diet. Tomatoes offer the carotenoid lycopene, which protects against breast and prostate cancers. And prunes are nature's miracle fruit—weight for weight, they supply the highest score of ORAC units (see page 13) of all foods. Just 3 1/2 ounces (about 13 prunes) will give you well over the optimum 5,000 protective units a day to prevent aging, degenerative disease, heart and circulatory problems, and, believe it or not, wrinkles.

Coconut fish

Serves 4

1 onion, finely chopped

1/2 fennel bulb, finely chopped

2 tablespoons olive oil

1 cup coconut milk

2 heaping tablespoons live
   natural yogurt

1/2 teaspoon grated nutmeg

1 teaspoon ground cumin

1 saffron strand

1 cup fish stock—see recipe for
   Fish with watercress (page 59)
   or use a good-quality, low-salt
   stock cube or bouillon powder

4 large tilapia (or red snapper)
   fillets or 8 smaller ones

1/4 cup chopped parsley

Coconut milk is a popular ingredient with the Jews of India, but this is a Sephardic recipe from Cuba. It is traditionally made with tilapia, a fish that comes from the Sea of Galilee. Christians believe the two large black marks on either side of the fish were left by the thumb and forefinger of St. Peter, hence its other name, St. Peter's fish. It's also popular in the cuisine of Arab countries, where it is known as *mousht*. And tilapia is the most widely used fish in Israel.

Serve with plain boiled rice and a tomato and scallion salad with Special vinaigrette (see page 82).

Method In a large heavy pan, gently sauté the onion and fennel in the oil until softened but not brown. Mix in the coconut milk, yogurt, nutmeg, cumin, saffron, and stock. Add the fish fillets, covering them with the coconut mixture.

Cover and simmer until the fish is cooked—about 10 minutes. Serve sprinkled with the parsley.

Health note This wonderfully healthy dish is virtually free from harmful saturated fat, is full of protein, calcium, and other minerals, and it tastes fabulous.

Herring in oatmeal

Serves 4

1/2 cup coarse oatmeal

4 grindings of black pepper

4 large herring, gutted and split
   (ask the person at the fish
   counter), washed and patted dry

1/4 cup (1/2 stick) unsalted butter

2 lemons, cut in half

Herring in all forms has been a staple food for Jews in Eastern and Northern Europe and in the UK. This recipe, from a Jewish family in Glasgow, is the ideal fusion of two cultures; the Scots also have herring as a staple part of their diet and they have the great tradition of using oats, one of the healthiest of all cereals.

Serve with cold Fava beans with beets and Magic mayonnaise with additions of your choice (see page 81) or warm baby potatoes boiled in their skins with Special vinaigrette (see page 82).

Method Mix together the oatmeal and pepper.

Lay the herring, skin side down, in a broiler pan and sprinkle generously with the oatmeal mixture. Dot with butter and broil under moderate heat for about 12 minutes. Put the lemon halves on the side of each plate for serving.

Health note No matter how you serve it, herring is the richest source of essential fatty acids, which are so important for brain development and function, as well as being naturally anti-inflammatory, and help relieve the problems of dyslexia, ADHD, and general learning difficulties in children. It also provides large amounts of the essential vitamin D, without which the body can't absorb calcium to build and maintain strong bones.

Opposite: Coconut fish

Hot and sour fish stew

Serves 4-6

*1 ounce (about a 1" cube) tamarind
pulp (available from speciaity
Indian food stores)*

2 tablespoons olive oil

1 white onion, finely chopped

2 tablespoons mild chili paste

Juice of 1 lime

*1 pound fresh salmon, pulled into
bite-sized pieces along the grain
of the flesh*

Whether they come from Eastern Europe, Persia, Palestine, or Israel, both Ashkenazi and Sephardi Jews have always enjoyed the combination of sweet and sour tastes. This recipe uses tamarind, traditionally thought of as an Indian ingredient, but equally at home in Jewish recipes in Iraq and Syria. Historically, tamarind pods have been used as much in Indian and Arabic medicine as they have in food. Preparing tamarind pulp from the commercially available dried blocks may seem like a lot of bother, but it's really worth the effort for its unique flavor.

Serve with Green beans with onion and thyme (see page 78) or a mixed-greens salad with Special vinaigrette (see page 82).

Method Put the tamarind pulp into a small bowl. Pour in a ½ cup of boiling water. Soak for about 20 minutes and push the pulp through a fine mesh strainer with a small wooden spoon.

Heat the oil in a large pan and gently sauté the onion until softened but not brown. Add the chili paste and cook gently, stirring continuously, for 5 minutes. Pour in the liquid from the tamarind pulp. Add the lime juice and bring to a simmer. Add the fish and stir until covered with the sauce. Cover and simmer gently until the fish is cooked—about 4-5 minutes.

Health note Heart-protective essential fatty acids from the salmon, and the circulatory stimulus from the chlli make this as healthy as it is tasty.

Trout in papaya sauce

Serves 4

8 fresh trout fillets

Juice of 1 lemon

1 tablespoon Tabasco sauce

1/4 cup flour, seasoned with
*   black pepper*

Scant cup of olive oil

2 papayas

2 tablespoons unsalted butter

1/2 cup dry white wine

Because of the demands of the Jewish dietary laws, Jews have developed interesting ways of preparing fish. Many less orthodox Jews are happy to eat in non-kosher restaurants or homes of non-Jewish friends, and although they wouldn't consume meat, fish would be acceptable.

A non-orthodox broadcasting colleague of mine is a keen fisherman whose freezer is always full of delicious trout. He's also an inventive cook and served this wonderful dish one very wet Sunday lunchtime. It is delicious with Eggplant rice (see page 91) or Pomegranate with avocado salad (page 75).

Method Put the fish in a large shallow dish.

Mix together the lemon juice and Tabasco sauce, pour it over the fish, cover, and let it marinate for at least 30 minutes. Take the fish out of the marinade and dust with the seasoned flour. Fry in the oil for about 3 minutes each side. Put onto a large plate and keep warm.

Mash the papaya flesh. Melt the butter gently in a clean pan. Add the wine and papaya flesh and warm gently, stirring continuously. Serve the fish with the papaya sauce on top.

Health note The heart and brain benefits of oily fish, the circulatory boost from the chili in the Tabasco sauce, and the enzymes and carotenoids from the papaya make this dish an excellent boost to your health as well as a delight to eat.

Spinach fish cakes with gooseberry sauce

Serves 4

12 ounces (about 1 1/2 cups) baby
    spinach leaves

1 cup mashed potatoes

12 ounces (about 1 1/2 cups) canned
    salmon (drained weight)

2 eggs

6 tablespoons medium matzo meal

About 2/3 cup canola (rapeseed) or
    sunflower oil for shallow frying

2 ounces (about 2–2 1/2 cups)
    gooseberries

2 tablespoons finely chopped mint

1 tablespoon honey

When I first left home to study in London, I shared a very primitive two-room flat with four friends. None of them had the faintest inkling of how to boil an egg, and we were all extremely hard-up. We put 10 shillings (that's half a pound sterling) a week into a kitty and, as I was the only one who could cook –allegedly–I had the job of feeding all five of us.

The best practical cook in my family was my Auntie Leah, my mother's unmarried sister, who was the peripatetic carer for the entire family. I used to phone her in desperation for ideas for nourishing meals, and this was her recipe for a cheap and cheerful alternative to the traditional fried *gefilte* fish. Everyone loved them and I still make them to this day. The sauce was a much later addition from my wife Sally when we had a glut of gooseberries in the garden.

Serve with cucumber salad made with peeled, thinly sliced cucumber drizzled with Special vinaigrette (see page 82) and sprinkled with finely chopped flat-leaf parsley.

Method Wash the spinach (even if it's "ready-washed"). Put into a large pot with just the water clinging to its leaves. Cover and heat, shaking occasionally, until just wilted. Chop roughly. Transfer to a large bowl with the potatoes and drained salmon, and mix well.

Beat the eggs in a shallow bowl. Put the matzo meal in another shallow bowl. Using your hands, mold the fish mixture into 8 burger shapes. Dip them first into the eggs, then into the matzo meal. Shallow fry, in batches, for 3 minutes each side. Keep warm.

Put the gooseberries into another pan with the mint. Add about 2/3 cup of water and the honey and simmer until the fruit becomes a pulp–about 10 minutes. Strain, pushing the fruit through a fine mesh strainer with a wooden spoon. Return to the pan and reheat gently.

Serve the fish cakes with the sauce on the side.

Health note There are wonderful nutrients in the spinach, energy from the mashed potatoes, essential fatty acids from the salmon, and fabulous fresh flavors in mint and gooseberries.

Chicken in orange sauce

Serves 6

6 plump chicken thighs, skin
  removed

Juice and finely chopped peel of
  2 large oranges

2 teaspoons ground turmeric

1 teaspoon black pepper

3 tablespoons olive oil

1 onion, finely chopped

2 garlic cloves, finely chopped

1 cup chicken broth—see
  recipe for Chicken soup with
  matzo dumplings (page 66), or
  use a good-quality, low-salt
  stock cube or bouillon powder

5 ounces, about 1 1/2 cups
  mushrooms, sliced

3 large sprigs of tarragon

You'd be forgiven for thinking that any form of poultry with orange sauce was part of the French *haute cuisine* tradition, but you'd be wrong. Jews have been cultivating citrus fruits since biblical times, as one of them, the citron (which looks like a very large lemon), is an essential part of the religious festival of Sukkot, the Feast of Tabernacles. Similar to the Christian harvest festival, it celebrates the produce of vineyards, fields, and orchards.

Although the citron has a wonderful aroma, it's not normally eaten raw, but the Jews became experts at growing other citrus fruits, which they took to ancient Rome, Spain, and the rest of the Mediterranean.

Serve with Spiced leeks (see page 71) or potatoes mashed with olive oil and chopped flat-leaf parsley.

Method Put the chicken pieces, orange juice and peel, turmeric, and pepper into a large bowl. Stir well to coat the chicken and leave covered in the fridge for at least 2 hours or overnight.

Heat the oil in a large heavy pan and gently sauté the onion and garlic until just starting to soften. Take the chicken pieces out of the marinade, add to the pan and brown all over, turning frequently. Add the marinade and broth and bring to a simmer. Add the mushrooms and tarragon. Simmer, covered, for about 45 minutes or until the chicken is tender.

Health note Oranges are widely used in Jewish cooking, and this low-fat recipe has the benefits of protein, vitamins, and essential oils from the orange skin as well as the cancer-fighting properties of turmeric.

Chicken with mango glaze

Serves 4

1 cup mango juice

4 plump scallions

1 tablespoon Dijon mustard

Leaves of 1 large sprig of rosemary

1 mango

4 chicken breasts

The history of Jews in Cuba is fascinating. The gradual demise of the Ottoman Empire, which was still in evidence until the First World War, and equal persecution of Jews and Muslims by Christians resulted in emigration from Turkey, the Balkans, Syria, and other parts of the Middle East. Some of these displaced people traveled to Cuba, where, whether they were Jews or Arabs, the Cubans lumped them all together as *turkos*. These turko-Sephardic Jews were at home with the Spanish language and customs, but in the 1920s there was an influx of Eastern European Jews whom the locals dubbed *polacos*. They ended up in Cuba because the USA placed strict quotas on immigrants fleeing the pogroms of Russia and Poland.

The small surviving community makes good use of local produce in their kosher cooking, and this recipe, which comes from Cuba, tastes great as well as containing huge amounts of protective antioxidants and essential nutrients. Serve with Turnips and carrots with garlic (see page 74) and wild rice.

Method Preheat the oven to 350°F. Put the mango juice, scallions, mustard, rosemary, and the flesh of the mango into a blender or food processor and whizz until smooth.

Put the chicken breasts into a large, shallow, ovenproof dish and drizzle with the mango mixture. Roast for about 40 minutes, basting frequently, until the chicken is thoroughly cooked.

Serve with the sauce poured over the chicken.

Squab chickens stuffed with chicken livers and veal

Serves 4

4 squab chickens

Olive oil

Salt and black pepper

1 onion, finely chopped

1/2 garlic clove, finely chopped

*8 ounces (about 1 cup) mixed veal
and chicken livers, ground up*

*2 heaping tablespoons fresh
bread crumbs*

1 teaspoon tomato paste

*1 tablespoon finely chopped
flat-leaf parsley*

*About 2/3 cup chicken broth—see
recipe for Chicken soup with
matzo dumplings (page 66) or
use a good-quality, low-salt stock
cube or bouillon powder*

I enjoyed a version of this recipe with Jewish friends who owned an ancient but working olive mill in the south of France. The chickens were free-range, and the French, because they've never subscribed to the intensive rearing of calves, are far less squeamish about eating veal.

Delicious with Sweet and sour zucchini (see page 71) and baby potatoes boiled in their skins.

Method Preheat the oven to 400°F. Drizzle the chickens with olive oil and sprinkle them with black pepper and a little salt. Roast for 20 minutes. While they're cooking, heat 2 tablespoons olive oil in a largish frying pan and gently soften the onion and garlic for 2 minutes. Add the veal and chicken livers and cook thoroughly for about 5 minutes. Add the bread crumbs, tomato paste, parsley, and some of the broth, and continue cooking, stirring continuously, for 3 minutes, adding more broth as necessary to get the consistency of a stuffing.

Use this mixture to stuff the cavities of the birds. Put them back into the oven, reduce the heat to 350°F, and roast for another 30 minutes.

Health note Rich in protein, iron, and B vitamins and very low in fat, this mixture of chicken, veal, and liver is a marriage made in the culinary heaven of France.

Chicken and chickpea curry

Serves 4

1/4 cup sesame oil

1 onion, finely chopped

3 garlic cloves, finely chopped

1 green chili, seeded and
   finely chopped

1 tablespoon curry powder

4 skinless chicken breasts, cut into
   strips along the grain of the meat

1-inch piece ginger root, peeled
   and grated

4 teaspoons tamarind paste

2 1/2 cups chicken broth—see
   recipe for Chicken soup with
   matzo dumplings (page 66)
   or use a good-quality, low-salt
   stock cube or bouillon powder

7 ounces (about 1 cup) canned
   chickpeas (drained weight),
   drained and rinsed

1/4 cup cilantro leaves, coarsely torn

It's possible that there were Jews in India by the end of the 12th century. There was an influx into India of Sephardi Jews, as you would expect, from Spain and Portugal, but also from Holland, where there was a large Jewish community during the 13th to 16th centuries. The Dutch were probably the most important spice traders in Europe, and it was India, this vast continent of spices, that presented great business opportunities to the Jews, who traded with the Dutch East India Company. During the 1980s, I worked in a clinic in one of the original canal-side spice warehouses, and you could still smell the lingering and evocative perfume of pepper, nutmeg, and cloves. One of the main areas in India in which all the Jews settled was Cochin, a southwestern coastal city and province, where they soon fused the local spices and cooking styles with their kosher traditions.

Although tamarind would have been a new taste for the Europeans, for those Jews who came much later from the Middle East, it was already a favorite flavoring. It adds an intriguing sweetness to this sharp curry and provides the added benefit of being a wonderful digestive aid.

Serve with Zucchini salad (page 86) and plain boiled rice.

Method Put the oil into a large pan. Gently sauté the onion, garlic, and chili until softened but not brown—about 5 minutes. Add the curry powder, mix thoroughly, and continue cooking for 2 minutes.

Add the chicken, ginger, and tamarind paste, and cook, stirring continuously, until the chicken is golden all over. Add the broth and simmer until the chicken is tender—about 35 minutes.

Stir in the chickpeas and cilantro and continue simmering until the chickpeas are heated through—about 7 minutes.

Roast duck with cherries

Serves 4

4 pounds oven-ready duckling

2 tablespoons olive oil

1 medium onion, finely sliced

1 heaping tablespoon flour

1 cup chicken broth—see
recipe for Chicken soup with
matzo dumplings (page 66) or
use a good-quality, low-salt stock
cube or bouillon powder

¼ cup port or kosher
dessert wine

1 tablespoon honey

1 pound (about 2 cups)
cherries, pitted

1 teaspoon ground cinnamon

1 star anise

Juice of 1 lemon

Duck and goose have always been part of Ashkenazi cooking throughout Eastern Europe and Germany, but duck was also a favorite in the Middle East and Asia. Some great recipes traveled with Jewish families who left Persia for Britain and America. This dish came from one of my aunt's Polish in-laws and is a firm favorite. Serve with Boulangère potatoes (see page 90) and Braised carrots (see page 85).

Method Preheat the oven to 425°F. Prick the duck all over with a fork. Cover loosely with foil and put on a trivet in a roasting pan containing at least an inch of boiling water. Roast for 15 minutes.

Remove from the oven and pour away the water and all the fat that has dropped into it. Take the duck off the trivet, return it to the roasting pan and put back into the oven. Reduce the heat to 350°F and continue roasting for another hour and 20 minutes (i.e., 20 minutes per pound).

Heat the oil in a saucepan and gently sauté the onion for 2 minutes. Mix in the flour, stirring well, and continue cooking over gentle heat for 2 more minutes. Add the broth, port or kosher dessert wine, honey, cherries, cinnamon, and star anise. Simmer until starting to thicken, stirring occasionally. Pour in the lemon juice and keep warm until the duck is cooked, carved, and ready to serve. Remove the star anise from the sauce and serve it poured over the duck.

Health note Although duck is perceived as being fatty, this cooking method removes most of the fat. As long as you don't eat the skin (delicious though it is), the end result is a low-fat dish full of iron, protein, and B vitamins. The cherries add wonderful flavor and an abundance of antioxidant phytochemicals.

Pigeons with juniper berries

Serves 4

About 6 tablespoons olive oil

12 pearl onions

3 slices of smoked beef, cut
*   into strips*

4 small pigeons

1 tablespoon flour

2 1/4 cups chicken broth—see
*   recipe for Chicken soup with*
*   matzo dumplings (page 66) or*
*   use a good-quality, low-salt stock*
*   cube or bouillon powder*

8 juniper berries, lightly crushed

3 large sprigs of parsley

2 sprigs of sage

2 bay leaves, broken in half down
*   the spine*

1 celery stalk, with leaves,
*   coarsely chopped*

Although goose was popular among the Ashkenazi Jews of Poland, and pigeon and quail were widely eaten in the Mediterranean, North Africa, and Egypt as part of the Sephardic tradition, these birds never seemed very popular with British Jewry. Certainly neither my mother, her sisters, nor any others in our vast extended family ever served them. Because of the requirements of ritual slaughter, game birds that had been shot weren't kosher—although quail and pigeon were traditionally caught or specially bred. Even duck was a rarity in Ashkenazi homes, although it was much more popular in the Sephardic culture.

You can substitute quail for the pigeons, but serve 2 per person—and the only way to eat these small birds is with your fingers. Serve with Red cabbage with apples and caraway (see page 70), Fava beans in olive oil (see page 73), and potatoes mashed with olive oil.

Method Heat the oil in a large flameproof casserole dish or other heavy pan, and sauté the onions until just colored—about 3 minutes. Add the smoked beef and continue cooking for another 3 minutes until the beef begins to turn brown. Remove the onions and beef from the pan. Adding more oil if necessary, brown the pigeons all over—2 at a time if your pan isn't large enough to move them around easily. Remove from the pan.

Sprinkle the flour into the remaining oil, mix thoroughly until well combined and gradually add the chicken broth, stirring continuously until thickened to a sauce. Pour into a heatproof measuring cup.

Put the onions and smoked beef back into the pan. Add half the sauce, along with the juniper berries, parsley, sage, bay leaves, and celery.

Arrange the pigeons on top and pour the remaining sauce over them. Cover tightly and simmer gently for about 50 minutes, until the pigeons are tender, adding extra broth or boiling water if the dish seems to be drying out. Put 1 pigeon on each plate and strain the sauce over the birds.

Health note This typically French recipe for pigeon casserole is extremely low in saturated fat—the type that clogs your arteries. The combination of pigeon and beef supplies substantial quantities of iron. As well as adding typical Mediterranean flavors, the juniper berries are a rich source of protective antioxidants. The onions are heart-protective and help reduce blood cholesterol. Sage improves digestion and bay leaves are a gentle mood-enhancer.

Beef loaf with tomato sauce

Serves 4

1 ½ pounds good-quality braising
  beef (such as chuck steak), all
  visible fat removed, ground up
8 ounces coarse matzo meal or 9
  matzo sheets, finely ground
1 onion, very finely chopped
2 eggs, beaten
1 tablespoon grated orange zest
1 tablespoon finely chopped mint
1 tablespoon flat-leaf parsley,
  finely chopped
½ teaspoon each ground
  cinnamon and ground cloves
2 dashes of Tabasco sauce
Canola (rapeseed) or sunflower oil,
  for greasing
1 cup beef stock—see recipe
  for Spiced lamb soup (page 64),
  but substitute beef for lamb, or
  use a good-quality, low-salt stock
  cube or bouillon powder
1 quantity Crushed tomato sauce
  (see page 95)

There's nothing particularly Jewish about meat loaf, but it is a very popular Jewish dish, particularly in Ashkenazi communities. Known throughout the Yiddish-speaking peoples as *klops*, it was a factor of economy and convenience. The cheapest cuts of beef could be used for grinding, and *klops* was a very practical dish as it could be eaten cold the following day with salad and a baked potato.

Although my mother's family all came from Eastern Europe, she made this Dutch *klops* for my father; the recipe comes from my grandmother who lived in Amsterdam. It's made here with very lean beef to reduce the fat content, and the mint makes it easily digestible while the cinnamon and cloves add the exotic flavor of the Dutch East Indies that permeates a lot of Dutch Jewish cooking.

This recipe goes well with Roast tomatoes with garlic (see page 83) and baby new potatoes boiled in their skins.

Method Preheat the oven to 350°F.

In a large bowl, mix together the beef, matzo meal, onion, eggs, orange zest, mint, parsley, ground cinnamon and cloves, and Tabasco sauce.

Heat the stock and keep it simmering.

Grease a 2-pound loaf pan (about 9 x 5 x 2³/4-inches) with a little oil—even if it's "non-stick." Put the meat mixture into the pan, packing it down firmly. Put the pan into a roasting pan half-filled with boiling water and bake for 40 minutes, pouring the hot stock over the meat as the loaf dries out.

Turn out onto a serving platter. Pour the Crushed tomato sauce over it for serving.

North African beef stew

Serves 6

1 calf's foot (optional)

3 tablespoons peanut oil

2 onions, finely sliced

2 garlic cloves, finely sliced

2 1/4 pounds lean stewing beef, cubed

12 new potatoes, unpeeled

2 large carrots, cubed

6 eggs, in their shells

12 ounces (about 2 1/4–2 1/2 cups) canned flageolet beans (drained weight)

2 teaspoons ground allspice

4 cups meat stock—see recipe for Spiced lamb soup (page 64) or use a good-quality, low-salt stock cube or bouillon powder

With the dominance of pre-packed supermarket food, people in northern Europe and the USA have grown increasingly separated from the reality of food. Children think milk comes from cartons, not cows, and fish sticks from the freezer, not the sea. It's hardly surprising, then, that we've become squeamish about what we eat. Variety meats, chicken's feet, calf's feet, and other "strange" bits and pieces are rarely used—which is sad as they're nutritious and usually inexpensive. Serve with Orange and olive salad (see page 77) and rice.

Method Preheat the oven to 350°F. Put the calf's foot, if using, into boiling water for 2 minutes, then drain.

Heat the oil in a large flameproof casserole dish or other heavy ovenproof pot and gently sauté the onions and garlic until softened but not brown—about 5 minutes. Add the calf's foot and the rest of the ingredients, including the eggs in their shells, and bring to a boil. Put into the oven for 2 hours, adding more stock if it dries out.

Serve with 1 hard-boiled egg on each plate. When shelled, the egg will be a rich brown color.

Health note Almost every cookbook written before the 1960s would have had a section on sick-room cooking—and that would have included calf's foot jelly, which is full of B vitamins, enzymes, and protein. Although optional in this recipe, do have a try. You'll be amazed by the delicate flavor and wonderful full-bodied texture it gives to this traditional Moroccan variation of *cholent*.

Lamb on couscous

Serves 6

1 1/2 pounds stewing lamb, cubed and all visible fat removed

5 cups lamb stock—see Spiced lamb soup (page 64) or use a good-quality, low-salt stock cube or bouillon powder

2 carrots, cubed

2 onions, finely sliced

2 zucchinis, cut into large cubes

1 turnip, cubed

3 cloves

3 bay leaves, broken in half

1/2 teaspoon sea salt or kosher salt

4 grindings of black pepper

2 tablespoons raisins

1 pound (about 2 2/3 cups) couscous

This combination of a savory meat dish with cloves is unmistakably Moroccan. If you imagine that the only place for cloves is in apple pie or in an orange to make mulled wine, you'll be missing out on one of the most distinctive flavors of this part of the world—served here with north African couscous. As long as you've trimmed the fat off the meat and skimmed the stock, this is a low-fat, high-protein meal which represents extremely good nutritional value for the money, with no compromise in taste. Good with Braised carrots (page 85).

Method Put the lamb into a large pot. Pour in the stock, bring to a boil and simmer, covered, until the lamb is tender—about 1 hour. Skim off any fat. Add the carrots, onions, zucchini, turnip, cloves, bay leaves, salt, pepper, and raisins. Simmer until the vegetables are cooked—about 10 minutes. Skim off any additional fat and keep the pot warm.

Cook the couscous according to package instructions, using stock from the pot instead of boiled water. Pile the couscous onto a large platter, with the lamb and vegetables arranged on top.

Health note Full of minerals and antioxidants from the root vegetables, and extra fiber and iron from the raisins, this is an ideal recipe for building stamina, strength, and natural immunity.

Lamb and lentils

Serves 4-6

4 lamb shanks (or 8 thick lamb
   chops)

1/4 cup olive oil

2 onions, finely sliced

1 large leek, thickly sliced
   diagonally

3 garlic cloves, finely sliced

3 large carrots, cut into large cubes

5 cups lamb stock—see recipe for
   Spiced lamb soup(page 64) or
   use a good-quality, low-salt stock
   cube or bouillon powder

9 ounces (about 1 1/3 cups) green
   or brown lentils

3 bay leaves

2 large sprigs of thyme

1 sprig of rosemary

The night before the Jews escaped in the great exodus from Egypt, their final meal was the Paschal lamb. Centuries later, Jews in every corner of the world remember this meal by the ritual of the roasted lamb shank (more likely to be a roasted chicken neck in modern homes), which is one of the symbolic foods displayed on the festive table of the Passover meal. Roasted lamb shank became a popular Jewish dish throughout the Middle East, and especially in Greece. Lentils were one of the earliest foods cultivated in "the promised land."

Serve with Beans in garlic (see page 78) and plain boiled rice.

Method Brown the lamb shanks (or chops) all over in the oil. Remove and set aside. Add the onions, leek, and garlic, and gently sauté until just softened. Add the carrots and continue to sauté for 5 minutes, stirring continuously.

Put the lamb and all the vegetables into a large heavy pot. Add the stock, lentils, bay leaves, thyme, and rosemary. Bring to a boil, then simmer for about 1 1/2 hours until everything is tender.

Remove the lamb, use a slotted spoon to pile the vegetables onto a large platter, and put the lamb on top. Pour the remaining stock into a gravy boat for serving.

Health note The lentils bring fiber, minerals, and B vitamins to the low-fat protein of this succulent dish.

Lamb and lemon kabobs with hot red salsa

Serves 6

1¹/2 pounds very lean ground lamb

Juice and grated zest of 1 large
 lemon

1 large egg (or 2 small ones), beaten

4 ounces fine matzo meal or 4
 matzo sheets, finely ground

1 teaspoon ground cumin

5 tablespoons finely chopped mint

5 tablespoons frozen corn,
 completely defrosted and
 crushed

1 red pepper, seeded and finely
 chopped

1 small red chile, seeded and
 finely chopped

2 tomatoes, finely chopped

2 shallots, finely chopped
 (if unavailable, use 1 small
 mild onion)

Whether you cook this under the broiler, in a grill pan or, best of all, on a barbecue, you'll enjoy the traditional taste of these Jewish/Egyptian lamb kabobs with the fiery heat of chiles: a taste that has spread from the North African Jews of Tunisia to communities in Yemen, India, South America, and finally back to Israel.

 This dish goes well with Nutty spinach with raisins (see page 88) and parboiled potato wedges brushed with olive oil and baked for about 20 minutes at 400°F.

Method Mix together the lamb, lemon juice and zest, egg(s), matzo meal, cumin, and half the mint. Roll into 18 small sausage shapes, thread onto kabob skewers and leave in the fridge for 30 minutes. Put under a hot broiler, or on a grill pan or barbecue, for about 10 minutes, according to size, until well cooked.

 While they're cooking, mix together the corn, red pepper, chile, tomatoes, and shallots. Serve the kabobs with the hot red salsa as a dip.

Health note This dish is full of health-promoting herbs and spices and is good for digestion, circulation, and blood pressure. It's the ultimate healthy alternative to the fast-food kabob.

Spiced lamb cutlets

Serves 4

8 lamb cutlets

4 onions, quartered

3/4 cup brown sugar

2/3 cup light soy sauce

1 teaspoon ground cinnamon

1 teaspoon ground cloves

4 generous grindings of black
  pepper

1/2-inch piece ginger root, peeled
  and grated

Adding these spices to a meat dish is typically north African and also popular in parts of the Middle East. This recipe clearly illustrates the difference between the Jewish cooking of middle and Eastern Europe and the Moorish influences on Jews who traveled in the opposite direction. In parts of the Middle East, this dish would be made with kid.

Serve with Roast tomatoes with garlic (see page 83) and baby new potatoes boiled in their skins.

Method Preheat the oven to 350°F. Put the cutlets into a large pan with the onions and just cover with water. Simmer gently for 10 minutes.

Meanwhile, heat the remaining ingredients gently in another saucepan.

Remove the cutlets and onions from their cooking liquid, add to the soy sauce mixture, coating thoroughly, and cook over very low heat for 10 minutes. Transfer the cutlets, without the soy sauce mixture, to an ovenproof dish and roast until crisp—about 30 minutes.

Health note It's low in fat, with lots of protein and all the medicinal benefits of the spices.

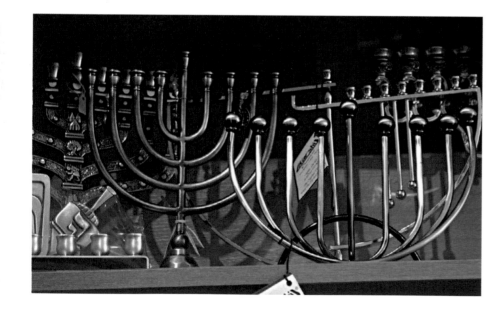

Veal schnitzel

Serves 4

2 medium eggs

1 teaspoon Worcestershire sauce

6 tablespoons fine matzo meal

1 teaspoon mustard powder

3-4 grindings of black pepper

4 veal cutlets, beaten thin
  between 2 sheets of plastic wrap
  with a meat mallet or rolling pin

¼ cup olive oil

1 lemon, quartered, for garnishing

During the 1920s and early 30s, German and Austrian Jews probably had the most influence on the whole of European Jewry. In fact, they considered themselves to be a cut above the rest, especially those of Eastern Europe. Many of their dishes were adopted and adapted by other communities, and the Wiener schnitzel, just like strudel and the other wonderful pastries of the coffee houses, spread from Vienna to Jews in Britain, France, Italy, Hungary, and across the Atlantic to America.

In recent years, there has been a resistance to eating veal because of the terrible conditions calves are often reared in. Try to find a kosher butcher who sells organic meat, the rearing of which forbids the use of crates, tethering, and other cruel practices. Serve with Lettuce with anchovies (see page 87).

Method Beat the eggs with the Worcestershire sauce. Mix together the matzo meal, mustard powder, and black pepper. Dip the cutlets in the egg mixture, then into the matzo meal. Fry in the oil until golden—about 2 minutes on each side. Garnish with the lemon quarters for serving.

Health note Veal has a very low fat content, as well as plenty of protein and B vitamins.

Calf's liver risotto

Serves 4

4 cups chicken broth—see recipe
    for Chicken soup with matzo
    dumplings (page 66) or use a
    good-quality, low-salt stock
    cube or bouillon powder

5 tablespoons olive oil

6 large scallions, cut into large
    chunks diagonally

10 ounces (about 1 1/2 cups) arborio
    or carnaroli rice

Black pepper

1 pound calf's liver, cut into strips

About 12 sage leaves, coarsely torn

This recipe originates from the Jews of northeast Italy and combines the two Italian culinary traditions of risotto and cooking liver with sage. It was the Arabs who first took rice to Italy, where it still grows abundantly on the marshy plains of the River Po.

All variety meats have traditionally been used widely in Jewish communities, but for most British and American Jews, liver, tongue, and possible kidneys are the only items that remain in common use. For the strictly orthodox, liver presents particular problems as it can't be rendered kosher by the traditional method of soaking and salting. To ensure that every last trace of blood is removed, the liver needs to be cooked over an open fire or under a very hot broiler within 72 hours of slaughtering and must not be allowed to sit in its own juices during cooking. The liver must be turned regularly and left exposed to the heat until it has cooked halfway through. Any liver that's going to be fried, baked, or cooked in any other way must go through this process first.

This recipe is lovely with Fava beans in olive oil (see page 73) or an avocado and romaine lettuce salad with Special vinaigrette (see page 82)

Method Pour the broth into a saucepan and bring to a gentle simmer.

Put 2 tablespoons of the oil into a large frying pan or wok and gently sauté the scallions until just soft—about 3 minutes. Add the rice and stir until all the grains are covered with oil. Ladle in about a quarter of the broth and stir vigorously until absorbed. Add the remaining broth, a ladleful at a time, still stirring until it has all been absorbed and the rice is just *al dente*. If necessary, add more broth or boiling water. Cover and keep warm.

Season the calf's liver with freshly ground black pepper and pan-fry quickly in the rest of the oil; it should take only about 1 minute, depending upon the size of the strips and your individual taste. Stir the liver gently into the rice, tip into a large bowl, and serve with the sage scattered on top.

Passover cup   Although this cup would have been used for only one week of the year, it was clearly important enough for the owner to want one to accommodate his moustache. Moustache cups were very popular in the Victorian period when men needed to protect their waxed moustaches. The inscription says "For the festival of Pesach" and it was probably added after purchase rather than incorporated into the original design.

desserts

Winter compôte

Serves 6

*8 ounces each (about 1 1/2 cups
  each) dried pitted
  prunes, dried apricots, dried
  pears, dried apples*

2 lemons, sliced

*1/4 cup each raisins, golden raisins,
  and slivered almonds*

*3 large pinches each of ground
  cinnamon and ground nutmeg*

1 tablespoon brandy (optional)

*2 1/2 cups freshly squeezed
  orange juice*

Dried fruits have always been popular in the Jewish kitchen. Dates, figs, and grapes have been dried in the Middle-Eastern sun since the earliest times and the techniques were adapted to local fruits wherever Jews settled. During the cold winter months, some alcohol was added to keep out the chill: in Poland it was plum brandy, in Italy, grappa, and in the UK (as in France) it was more likely to be brandy.

This is a perfect dessert for the kosher kitchen as it can be eaten at any time of the day, with meat or fish meals, and, of course, can be cooked on Friday to be used on the Sabbath. When it is not eaten before or after meat, crème fraîche is an ideal accompaniment, into which you stir 1/3 cup orange juice and 1 tablespoon brandy (optional).

Method Preheat the oven to 350°F. Mix together the dried prunes, apricots, pears, and apples, and put half in the bottom of a large casserole dish. Cover with half the lemon slices. Mix together the raisins, golden raisins, and almonds, and sprinkle half on the lemon layer. Repeat layers, using the remaining fruit and nuts. Sprinkle with the cinnamon and nutmeg.

Mix together the brandy, if using, and the orange juice, and pour them over the dish. Bake for 20 minutes.

Health note Although even biblical Jews understood that dried fruits were healthy, they couldn't have imagined the enormous protective value of this compôte. Each portion provides an entire day's dose of ORAC units (see page 13), which protect against aging, cell damage, cancers, and even wrinkles. Vitamins, minerals, and instant energy from the fruit sugars abound, and there's even a little protein and vitamin E from the almonds. Not even my mother would have understood the mood-enhancing benefits of nutmeg or the antibacterial properties of cinnamon—but there was always a bowl of this winter dessert in our fridge.

Matzo fritters with rosewater syrup

Serves 4-6

1/2 cup sugar

1/4 cup honey

Juice and grated zest of 1 lemon

1/2 cup rosewater

4 eggs

6 tablespoons medium matzo meal

About 2 cups canola (rapeseed) or sunflower oil

Passover is a wonderful time of the year. I still remember the excitement of all the preparation, the hours spent watching my mother and her sisters creating all the special cakes and cookies made with strange (to a child, at least) ingredients such as potato flour, ground almonds, and coconut, and the disasters caused by banging any door in the house while the special Passover cake, *plaver*, was in the oven. It all culminated on the evening before Passover in the search for *chametz*—bread and cakes.

During Passover, no leavened bread must be eaten, and nothing containing even a trace of leavening is allowed to remain in the house. So, armed with a candle and a feather, my mother would search the nooks and crannies of the kitchen so that any minute crumbs could be swept up and ceremoniously burned. For the next seven days, only unleavened bread—called *matzo*, "the bread of affliction," eaten by the Jews when they escaped from Egypt as there was no time to let the dough rise—was allowed.

At least today you can find whole-wheat matzo, which makes life a little easier as many people find normal matzo constipating. There are many recipes for cooking with matzo. Here's my favorite, with the exotic Ottoman flavor of rosewater.

Method Put the sugar, honey, and 3 tablespoons lemon juice into a pan with a scant cup of water. Bring to a boil, stirring, until the sugar and honey are dissolved. Add the rosewater and set aside but keep warm.

Separate the eggs and whisk the whites until stiff. In another bowl, beat the yolks gently with the lemon zest and fold into the whites. Sift the matzo meal over the whisked eggs, then mix thoroughly.

Heat the oil in a large, wide frying pan. Drop in the fritter mixture a tablespoon at a time and shallow-fry, turning once, until golden; you'll have to do this in batches. As you're cooking, drain each batch of fritters on paper towels and keep warm. Arrange the warm fritters on a serving dish and pour the rosewater syrup over them.

Baked apples stuffed with figs

Serves 4

4 large dessert apples

8 dried figs, chopped

2/3 cup apple juice

1 tablespoon honey

2 tablespoons unsalted butter

There is certainly no sin in eating these apples and, combined in this popular Jewish dessert with all the traditional health-giving benefits of figs, they are delicious served with sherbet or kosher non-dairy ice cream.

Method Preheat the oven to 400°F. Cut a slice off the bottom of the apples so that they stand upright. Remove the cores with an apple corer. Cut a 1/2-inch off the end of each core and replace in the apples to form a plug.

Cover the figs with boiling water and let stand for 5 minutes. Drain, reserving the liquid. Pack the figs into the apples and put them into a roasting pan. Mix together the fig liquid, apple juice, honey, and butter, and pour it over the apples. Cover the pan with foil and bake for 20 minutes.

Remove the foil and bake for another 15 minutes.

Health note Apples are rich in pectin, a form of soluble fiber that helps reduce cholesterol, while figs contain anti-cancer agents, healing enzymes, and digestion-improving natural chemicals.

Soy rice pudding with Brazil nut compôte

Serves 6

3 ounces (about 1/3 cup)
    short-grain rice

1 3/4 cups soy milk

4 cardamom seeds, smashed with
    a rolling pin

About 1/4 cup (1/2 stick)
    unsalted butter

2 ounces (about 1/3 cup) Brazil
    nuts, ground (if unavailable, use
    macadamia nuts instead)

1 tablespoon honey

2 tablespoons freshly squeezed
    orange juice

Opposite: *Baked apples stuffed
with figs*

Neither rice, soy milk, nor Brazil nuts were around at the beginning of Jewish history, but Jewish cooks are nothing if not inventive and adventurous. For people keeping kosher, soy milk is an excellent alternative to cow's milk and can be used in many milk-based recipes which can't normally be eaten as part of, or soon after, a meat meal.

This recipe, however, would not be kosher with a meat meal because of its use of butter, which is what makes rice pudding so delicious. From a health point of view, I'm not an admirer of any margarine, but if you're keeping kosher and wish to benefit from the great health benefits of this dessert, substituting a little kosher margarine would be acceptable if you wanted to serve this after a meat meal.

Mixing nuts, honey, and cardamoms is a traditional feature of Sephardic cooking, but this is a universal recipe we created for this book.

Method Preheat the oven to 300°F. Put the rice, soy milk, and cardamoms into a large ovenproof dish greased with a little butter. Dot with the remaining butter. Bake for about 1 1/2 hours.

Mix together the Brazil nuts, honey, and juice. Serve each bowl of rice with a spoonful of nut compôte on top.

Pears in black currant sauce

Serves 4-6

*A tiny amount of unsalted butter
(or canola or sunflower oil if
you're keeping kosher and want
to eat this after a meat meal)*

4 Bosc pears, cut in half

Juice of 1 lemon

2 tablespoons brown sugar

*1 pound black currants, fresh or
defrosted, from frozen*

1 tablespoon honey

¼ cup sweet white wine

In some Eastern European Jewish communities, particularly in Poland and Hungary, mixing fruit and wine made some of the most popular desserts. Here, the last of the season's fresh currants combine with the first of the autumn pears. The contrast of the sharp and sweet flavors makes a delicious end to a healthy meal.

Method Preheat the oven to 350°F. Using as little butter as possible, grease an ovenproof dish large enough to take the pears in one layer. Place the pears in the dish, cut side down. Pour the lemon juice over them and add enough water to come halfway up the sides of the fruit. Sprinkle with the sugar. Cover and bake until the pears are just tender, about 30 minutes, until the fruit is soft and crinkly. Drain and return the pears to the dish.

While the pears cook, put the black currants, honey, and wine into a blender and whizz until smooth. (For an extra-smooth sauce, you may want to strain it through a fine mesh strainer.) Pour the mixture evenly over the drained pears, cover, and bake for another 20 minutes. Chill before serving.

Health note Currants are the richest source of vitamin C and antioxidants, and the pears provide the valuable fiber known as pectin.

Blackberry and apple crisp

Serves 6

1 pound (about 3 medium) tart
  dessert apples (like Granny
  Smith)

1 pound (about 3 1/2 cups)
  blackberries (fresh are best, but
  defrosted frozen fruit will work)

2 teaspoons brown sugar

6 ounces (about 1 3/4–2 cups)
  ground almonds

6 ounces (about 1 2/3 cups)
  rolled oats

2 tablespoons honey

3 tablespoons slivered almonds

1/3 cup (3/4 stick) unsalted butter,
  finely cubed

Oats weren't around in biblical times, although the wild oat was probably the source of the early cultivated oats in central Europe. The most successful species weren't widely used until the end of the 18th century, when they became popular in the poorest communities of Europe and the UK. Oats also found a ready home in the cooking of most Ashkenazi Jews, and today they are often used in cookies, mixed with other flours to make bread and pancakes, and eaten as breakfast cereals.

Thick whole-milk live plain yogurt makes a good accompaniment.

Method Preheat oven to 400°F. Peel, core, and slice the apples. Put into a lightly buttered baking dish and scatter with the blackberries. Sprinkle with the sugar and add 2 tablespoons water.

Mix together the ground almonds and oats and sprinkle them over the fruit. Drizzle with the honey, scatter the slivered almonds on top and dot with the butter. Bake for 30 minutes.

Health note Comparatively low in saturated fats and immensely rich in vitamins, minerals, the best sort of fiber and protective antioxidants, this is a dessert to be enjoyed at all times of the year, but the apples, honey, and almonds make it a healthy alternative to a traditional autumn fruit crumble.

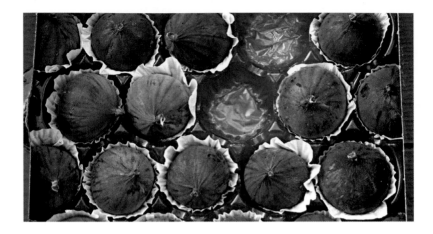

Olive fig tart

Serves 4-6

For the olive-oil pastry dough
1 2/3 cups all-purpose flour
1 cup minus 2 tablespoons olive oil
1 egg, beaten
1 teaspoon brown sugar

For the filling
12 fresh, ripe figs
1/4 cup heavy cream
1/2 cup live plain yogurt
1 teaspoon almond extract
2 tablespoons honey

What could be more biblical than this combination which includes oil from olives, and figs and honey? The Old Testament abounds with mentions of all three, and the fig tree is a powerful image in Judaism: from the leaves that clothed Adam and Eve to the times of happiness and prosperity, safety and security represented by the biblical description of living under one's own fig tree.

Figs are among the most abundant fruits in the Middle East and in southern Europe. They are widely used in the cooking of orthodox Jews in Greece, Italy, and Turkey, and they were extremely popular with the Sephardim, who usually finished their meals with fruit. Sacred to Hindus, Buddhists, and the ancient Greeks and Romans, figs were regarded as both food and medicine.

Method To make the pastry dough, put all the pastry ingredients into a food processor and blend, using the kneading blade, until they make a dough—about 2 minutes. Mold into a ball, wrap in plastic and leave in the fridge for at least 1 hour.

Preheat the oven to 350°F. Lightly grease a 9-inch removable-bottomed fluted tart pan. Use the dough to line the tart pan, and prick lightly with a fork all over. Line the dough with baking parchment, cover with dried beans, and bake for 10-15 minutes. Remove the beans and paper and bake for 5 more minutes to crisp the crust.

Cut the figs in half lengthwise and arrange on the crust. Whisk together the cream, yogurt, almond extract, and honey. Pour it over the figs and bake for 50 minutes, until the cream mixture is set. Serve warm or cold but not chilled.

Health note With no saturated fat, the health-giving benefits of olive oil, calcium from the yogurt, and the unique cancer-protective chemicals and enzymes in figs, this is a great dessert, which actually improves digestion after a meal rather than lying heavily on the stomach.

Cinnamon-baked plums with orange mascarpone sauce

Serves 6

Unsalted butter, for greasing

12 French prune plums, or other sweet, small eating plums cut in half and pitted

About 1 cup full-bodied red wine

3 cinnamon sticks

2 tablespoons brown superfine sugar

1/3 cup freshly squeezed orange juice

1 cup mascarpone cheese

1 large sprig (about 12 leaves) of mint, leaves coarsely torn

This succulent dessert came originally from a Jewish friend who lives in the Agen region of France, where it is made with the unique prune plums, *pruneaux d'Agen*, before they're dried to make the best prunes in the world. Victoria plums were the best alternative we could find in England, and the result was a light, delicately flavored, and healthy dessert—the perfect end to any meal.

Method Preheat the oven to 400°F. Generously butter a large pie dish and lay the plums, cut side down, on top. Pour in the wine, add the cinnamon, and sprinkle with the sugar. Cover with foil and bake until the plums are soft—about 25 minutes.

Gently mix the orange juice and mascarpone together. Serve with the mint leaves scattered over the plums and the mascarpone sauce on the side.

Health note The red wine brings cardio-protective benefits and there is lots of potassium from the plums as well as a little vitamin E and an abundance of protective antioxidants to help fight aging. With extra protein and calcium from the mascarpone and the digestive properties of mint, this is a fighting-fit dessert.

Stuffed prunes with coconut sauce

Serves 4

1 cup red wine

1 tablespoon honey

16 pitted ready-to-eat prunes

16 whole almonds, shelled

2/3 cup coconut milk

Every Jewish comedian will have at least one joke in his repertoire about constipation and the popularity of prunes in Ashkenazi cooking. While there's no doubt that prunes can have a laxative effect, this is greatly over-estimated as you need to eat around twelve of these highly nutritious dried fruits at one sitting for this to happen.

Method Put the wine into a wide-bottomed pan, add the honey, and heat, stirring constantly, until dissolved.

Make a lengthwise cut halfway through each prune and insert an almond into each cavity, pressing the sides of the prune gently to close. Place carefully in the wine mixture, in a single layer. Bring the wine to a boil and simmer for 15 minutes. Remove the prunes and place in a serving dish.

Boil the wine until slightly reduced. Add the coconut milk and heat gently. Pour the sauce over the prunes for serving.

Health note Prunes are exceptionally rich in potassium, fiber and, above all, protective antioxidants. In fact, weight for weight, they have the highest ORAC score (see page 13) of all foods. Extra protein and vitamins from the almonds and the aromatic essence of coconut milk make this dish extremely healthy as well as delicious.

Opposite: *Cinnamon-baked plums with orange mascarpone sauce*

Cherry clafoutis

Serves 4

About ¼ cup (½ stick) unsalted
butter

18 ounces (about 2–2 ½ cups)
black cherries, pitted

1 tablespoon finely chopped lemon
balm leaves or lemon verbena (if
unavailable, use ½ tablespoon
dried verbena or ½ tablespoon
lemon zest

3 eggs

⅓ cup plain whole-wheat flour

1 ¾ cups low-fat milk

Clafoutis started life as a specialty in France, where it was most popular in the Limousin region. With the Jewish love of sweet fruits combined with cake, it soon became a favorite among French Jews, who rapidly took it to other parts of Europe.

Method Preheat the oven to 400°F. Grease a large, shallow, ovenproof dish with a little of the butter. Put the cherries into the dish along with the lemon balm.

Whisk the eggs. Melt the remaining butter and whisk into the eggs. Still whisking, sift in the flour, then add the milk. Pour the egg mixture over the cherries and bake until set—about 45 minutes.

Health note Black cherries are another of the dark-colored fruits that are rich in antioxidants, and they have the added benefit of bioflavonoids, substances that specifically protect the linings of blood vessels. Adding the lemon balm not only imparts a unique flavor, but also makes this dish calming, mood-enhancing, and, interestingly, will give you special protection against viral infections, particularly cold sores and other variations of herpes—a property unique to lemon balm.

Coconut bread pudding with strawberries

Serves 6-8

6 large but thin slices of panettone

1 pound (about 3 ¹/₂–4 cups)
*   strawberries, hulled and cut in*
*   half (or quartered if large)*

3 cups coconut milk

4 cups sugar, plus extra
*   for sprinkling*

1 tablespoon Amaretto

5 eggs, lightly beaten

Masters of "fusion" cooking before it was even heard of, British Jews soon adopted and adapted many traditional dishes, including bread-and-butter pudding. Borrowing from the tropics, they even used coconut milk and kosher margarine so that orthodox Jews could eat this dish with a meat meal. My favorite is this Italian version cooked by a non-Jewish friend who'd lived and worked in Italy for some years. Many Jews, who of course don't celebrate Christmas, invite non-Jewish friends to enjoy a traditional, but kosher, Christmas meal. This recipe makes a much lighter and healthier alternative to Christmas pudding.

Method Preheat the oven to 350°F. Put 2 slices of the panettone into a casserole dish, cutting it to fit snugly. Scatter half the strawberries over it. Top with 2 more slices of panettone, the rest of the strawberries, then the final 2 slices of panettone. Put the coconut milk into a pan along with the sugar and stir over low heat until the sugar is dissolved. Add the Amaretto. Let cool slightly and beat in the eggs.

Pour the mixture over the panettone and strawberries and sprinkle the extra sugar on top. Bake for 45 minutes, until golden.

Health note It may not look hugely healthy, but per serving this dish is low in fat and full of protective antioxidants and vitamins from the strawberries, and contains very modest amounts of sugar.

Ginger lemon sherbet

Serves 6

2 teaspoons ginger extract,
   (if unavailable use 2 teaspoons
   juice squeezed from freshly
   grated gingeroot)
³/4 cup sugar
Juice of 2 large (or 3 smaller)
   lemons
Lavender cookies (see page 146),
   for serving

Sorbets (sherbets) have long been a favorite in all Jewish communities. Because dairy ice cream cannot be eaten as part of a kosher meat meal, fruit-based water ices are wonderful, refreshing, and palate-cleansing alternatives. Particularly in the Ashkenazi societies in the UK and North America, the water ice has become a bit of a joke as it's nearly always served during elaborate banquets at weddings and bar mitzvahs.

Method Put the ginger extract and sugar into a saucepan with 1³/4 cups cold water. Bring slowly to a boil, stirring to dissolve the sugar, and simmer for 3 minutes. Cool completely and add the lemon juice.

   Put into an ice cream or sherbet maker and follow the machine instructions. Alternatively, put into a bowl and leave in the freezer until half-frozen. Whisk until smooth and return to the freezer. Repeat the whisking and freezing routine once more.

   Leave in the freezer until needed. Serve with Lavender biscuits.

Health note This sherbet is rich in vitamin C, with the added benefit of circulatory stimulation from the ginger.

Ginger soufflé

Serves 4

Olive oil, for greasing

2 tablespoons unsalted butter

2 tablespoons flour

¼ cup ginger syrup (from a jar of preserved ginger), plus 4 pieces of preserved ginger, finely sliced, for serving

½ cup milk

2 tablespoons brown sugar

3 egg yolks

4 egg whites

2 pinches of ground ginger

Of all the spices, ginger is probably the best-loved in Jewish cooking. In the Sephardic tradition, it's often used in savory dishes just as it is in the Middle East, Far East, China, and India, whereas Ashkenazi cooks use it mostly in sweet dishes such as cakes, cookies, puddings, and ice cream.

Method Preheat the oven to 400°F. Brush a 7-inch soufflé dish with olive oil. Cut a sheet of parchment paper long enough to go completely around the outside of the dish and deep enough to stand 4 inches taller than the rim. Grease the paper and tie it around the outside of the dish, greased side facing inwards.

Melt the butter in a pan over low heat. Gradually add the flour, stirring continuously, until combined. Mix together the ginger syrup and milk. Still stirring continuously, add the ginger syrup and milk to the flour mixture and heat gently until thickened. Remove from the heat and beat in the sugar.

Separate the eggs and beat the 3 yolks separately into the soufflé mixture. In a clean bowl and using a clean beater, beat all 4 whites until stiff and fold them into the soufflé with a metal spatula or spoon.

Put the dish into a roasting pan and add enough boiling water to come about an inch up the side of the dish. Bake for 30 minutes until risen and golden. Remove the paper sleeve, sprinkle with the ground ginger, and serve with the preserved ginger slices on the side.

Health note It is stretching credibility to describe any soufflé as truly healthy, but this is about as good as they get. There's calcium and vitamins in the milk; protein, more vitamins, and iron in the eggs; and the natural chemicals in the ginger provide a substantial boost to the circulatory system.

Persian fruit salad

Serves 8

3 bananas, peeled and sliced

3 oranges, peeled, segmented, and
    all inner skin removed

2 apples, peeled, cored, and cubed

1 cup dates, chopped

1 cup prunes, chopped

1 cup dried figs, chopped

1 cup freshly squeezed orange juice

Juice of 1 lime

1/2 cup orange-flower water

1/4 cup chopped almonds

Lavender cookies (see page 146),
    for serving

This is another typical Sephardic fruit recipe, which combines fresh and dried fruits. One of the most famous Indian chefs in London, Cyrus Todiwala, told me that his favorite functions are Persian weddings because of the piles of luscious fresh and dried fruits used in so many recipes. They're equally loved by Persian Muslims, Christians, and Jews.

This dish was traditional on the Jewish festival of Tu B'Shvat, which occurs on the 15th day of the Jewish month of *Shvat*. In the Western calendar, this happens in January or February, which may seem a little strange, as in Hebrew the festival is called the "New Year for Trees," but this is when trees begin to sprout in Israel. Tu B'Shvat's praise of all the biblical species of figs, dates, pomegranates, olives, and grapes signifies that healthy trees bear fruit. For orthodox Jews, this festival teaches that man, too, should "bear fruit" in the form of good deeds.

Method Put all the fruit (fresh and dried) into a large bowl. Mix together the orange and lime juice and orange-flower water, pour them over the fruit, and turn gently until well combined, ensuring the bananas are especially well covered with the juice: this prevents them from browning. Leave for at least 2 hours. Sprinkle with the chopped almonds and serve with Lavender cookies.

Health note Delicious, energizing, nourishing, and hugely protective, this is one dessert that should be eaten throughout the year.

Matzo tools
Cakes and cookies are an intrinsic part of the Jewish culinary tradition. If you go into any Jewish house in the afternoon—except, of course, on the Sabbath—you'll smell the aroma of baking. These wonderful iron tools were almost certainly from the late 19th century and used for stamping and punching unleavened bread. Although matzo is now generally available throughout the year, it used to be made especially for Passover and there are a whole set of rules governing its production. These implements would have only been used for Passover matzo making.

cookies and cakes

Basic cookies

Makes about 12 cookies

1/2 cup (1 stick) unsalted butter or
  kosher margarine or 1/2 cup
  olive oil
1/2 cup brown sugar
1 egg yolk
4 drops vanilla extract
2/3 cup self-rising
  whole-wheat flour
1 cup self-rising white flour
2 1/2 teaspoons baking powder
3/4 teaspoon salt

Baking lies at the heart of the Jewish kitchen as cakes and cookies of all sorts are an integral part of social activities and religious festivals. One of the great traditions of Ashkenazi baking is *kichles* (or *kichlach*), always served with wine and other alcoholic drinks after synagogue services and all social gatherings. My mother's original recipe used white flour and butter, but over the years I was able to point her gently in the direction of healthier cooking and she ended up using a mixture of whole-wheat and white flour.

There are many variations of this basic recipe. You could try sandwiching 2 cookies together, flat side down, with low-sugar marmalade to make "Jaffa cakes"; adding 3 pinches of ground ginger, cinnamon, or allspice to the flour; or brushing the uncooked cookies with a little beaten egg white and sprinkling with dried coconut or caraway seeds.

Method Preheat the oven to 400°F. Cream together the butter or margarine or oil, and the sugar. Beat in the egg yolk and vanilla extract.

Sift in the dry ingredients, mix well, and knead to a dough. On a floured surface, roll out to about a 1/4 inch thick and cut into any shapes you like (for children, you could make cut-outs of their names, for example). Put onto a lightly greased cookie sheet and bake until golden—about 15 minutes.

Ginger hazelnut cookies

Serves 8-10

3/4 cup brown sugar
8 ounces (about 2 cups) hazelnuts,
  ground
2 ounces (about 1/2 cup) walnuts,
  ground
1 teaspoon ground ginger
1 teaspoon ground cloves
2 large eggs, beaten
Rice flour, for dusting

Ginger originates from the warmer regions of Asia and was used as both food and medicine in China more than 5,000 years ago. The ancient Greeks and Romans used ginger, but even before then it appeared in the earliest Sanskrit writings. One of the many spices loved in the Sephardi world, it was important to Muslims as well because of its warming properties. Islamic Paradise is said to have two fountains: one with ginger, for warming, the other with camphor, for cooling.

Method Preheat the oven to 350°F. Mix together the sugar, nuts, and spices. Add the eggs and beat in well.

Lightly grease a cookie sheet and, using a tablespoon, put mounds of the mixture on it. Bake until golden—about 30 minutes. Serve cold, dusted lightly with rice flour.

Health note Popular in most of north Africa, especially Morocco, and of course widely used in Chinese cooking, ginger stimulates the circulation and is the best of all remedies for nausea and sickness. Combined here with the protein and minerals from nuts and the digestive help from cloves, this Greek Jewish recipe is not only delicious, but is also ideal to combat travel sickness and early-morning sickness in the first stages of pregnancy.

Orange-scented pine nut and sesame snaps

Serves 4–6

*1/2 cup mixed pine nuts and
     sesame seeds*

*1 cup raw sugar (if unavailable, use
     light brown)*

1/4 cup orange-flower water

Juice of 1/2 lime

1 teaspoon ground allspice

Although this is a favorite sweet treat in Israel, the origins of sesame seeds lie in the Balkans, the Far East, and India. Sesame seed oil was also used in India, Iraq, and Syria, and sesame is the main ingredient of the traditional Middle Eastern sweet *halva*.

Method Dry-fry the pine nuts and sesame seeds until golden. Put the sugar into a saucepan along with the orange-flower water, lime juice and a 1/3 cup of water. Stir over gentle heat until the sugar has dissolved, then simmer until thick and golden. Add the pine nuts, sesame seeds, and allspice, and heat through gently for about 2 minutes. Pour onto a cold, damp surface and roll with a rolling pin until about a 1/2-inch thick.

   Cut into bars about an inch wide and 4 inches long and transfer, using a spatula, to a cold, clean surface. Let harden before serving.

Health note Like all confectionery, these snaps are high in sugar, so should be regarded as a treat, but even so, the minerals, mono-unsaturated fats, and vitamin E content of the seeds and nuts are extremely nutritious. Sesame seeds contain valuable quantities of bone-building calcium, so they're useful for anyone who doesn't eat dairy products.

Lavender cookies

Serves 4

1/4 cup brown sugar

1/2 cup (1 stick) unsalted butter

1/4 cup whole-wheat flour

1 3/4 teaspoons baking powder

1/2 teaspoon salt

*12 tablespoons chopped lavender
leaves*

*2 teaspoons lavender flowers,
stripped from their stems*

These aren't traditional Jewish cookies, but they should be as they use every Jewish cook's basic cookie method of *kichles*. They go particularly well with the rather sweet kosher red wine produced in Israel.

This recipe works equally well with fresh rosemary leaves—and rosemary flowers if you can get them or if you grow your own. If using rosemary, add 2 tablespoons freshly grated Parmesan to the flour before mixing into the dough. Essential oils in rosemary have a specific effect on the brain and improve the memory.

Method Preheat the oven to 425°F. Cream together the sugar and butter. Add the remaining ingredients (except the lavender flowers) and knead into a dough. Roll out on a floured board, sprinkle with the flowers, and press them into the dough with a rolling pin. Cut with a smallish cookie cutter, about 2$1/2$ inches in diameter, or into squares or any other shape you like.

Put onto a greased cookie sheet and bake until golden—about 10 minutes.

Health note Stress and anxiety seem to be the traditional collective problem of Jewish mothers around the world, and the addition of lavender to this recipe makes these cookies calming, mood-enhancing, and very slightly soporific.

Peanut butter squares

Serves 8-10

2/3 cup whole-wheat flour

1 cup white flour

2 1/2 teaspoons baking powder

3/4 teaspoon salt

1 teaspoon ground ginger

*3 tablespoons crunchy peanut
butter*

2 tablespoons honey

*3 tablespoons shelled, unsalted
peanuts*

Here's a surprisingly healthy addition to your baking repertoire. Most people think of peanuts and peanut butter as being fattening and unhealthy when in fact they're quite healthy indeed.

Method Preheat the oven to 350°F. Mix together the dry ingredients. Rub in the peanut butter until the mixture has the texture of bread crumbs.

Warm the honey and stir well into the mixture. Knead to a dough and roll out on a floured board.

Dry-fry the peanuts and press firmly into the dough. Cut the dough into 2-inch squares. Transfer to a lightly greased cookie sheet and bake for 20 minutes. Serve cold.

Health note Peanuts aren't only a valuable component of any weight-loss program because they have a low glycemic index (which means they're broken down very slowly into sugars and consequently have little effect on insulin levels), but they also help prevent diabetes. They're a rich source of mono-unsaturated fats, which help the body eliminate cholesterol, and they're rich in protein, vitamins, and minerals. The combination of peanuts and whole-wheat flour in this recipe also provides valuable amounts of fiber.

Opposite: *Lavender cookies*

Cinnamon balls

Serves 4-6

3 egg whites

1 heaping tablespoon ground cinnamon

5 ounces ground almonds (about 1 2/3 cups)

7 ounces brown sugar (about 1 cup)

Rice flour, for dusting

At the time of Passover, the total absence of bread and the resulting dependence on *matzo* were only endurable by all my young cousins and me because of the abundance of these cinnamon balls. My mother's youngest sister, Gertie, was the cinnamon-ball maker and she produced them by the tinful for the entire family.

These are perfect for anyone who's a celiac or who suffers from wheat intolerance. They're normally dusted with confectioners' sugar to prevent them from sticking together, but I prefer to use rice flour instead as it doesn't increase the sugar content. Ideally, these balls should be firm on the outside, but soft and succulent in the middle. Overcooked, they turn into tooth-breakers.

Method Preheat the oven to 350°F.

Beat the egg whites until very stiff. Add the cinnamon, almonds, and sugar and mix well. Roll the mixture into balls about the size of a large plum, set on a greased cookie sheet and bake until set—about 30 minutes.

Dust with the rice flour before setting aside to cool.

Health note Though high in sugar, these cinnamon balls are rich in protein, vitamin E, minerals, and the antibacterial benefits of cinnamon.

Rice and cheese bake

Serves 4-6

Both sheets from 17-ounce package of frozen puff pastry, or make your own

2 cups cooked short-grain rice

14 ounces low-fat cream cheese (about 1 3/4 cups)

2 eggs, beaten

1 tablespoon raw sugar

3 tablespoons plump golden raisins

Rice pudding is one of the most popular desserts in Portugal, and this Jewish recipe from Lisbon would have been traditionally prepared with homemade curd cheese. It provides protein, calcium, iron, and fiber and combines the Sephardi favorites of rice, cheese, and dried fruits.

Method Preheat the oven to 350°F.

Roll out the pastry dough and use it to line a greased 11 x 8-inch baking pan. Mix together the rice, cheese, eggs, sugar, and raisins. Put the mixture into the pie shell.

Bake until the pastry is golden and the filling set—about 35 minutes.

Opposite: *Cinnamon balls*

Navy bean cake

Serves 4-6

3 large eggs
3/4 cup brown sugar
10 ounces (about 1 3/4–2 cups) navy
beans, cooked, rinsed, drained,
and left until completely cold
Juice and grated zest of 1 large
lemon
2 tablespoons Amaretto (optional)
3 tablespoons ground almonds,
for serving

Beans have always been popular in Jewish cooking as an addition to casseroles, soups, and stews, but it's only among the Sephardi community that they're used in sweet dishes, too. This Middle Eastern cake may sound strange, but it tastes wonderful and is an interesting alternative to the usual Ashkenazi recipes baked during Pesach when no flour is allowed.

Method Preheat the oven to 350°F. Separate the eggs, reserving the whites, and beat the yolks into the sugar. Mix in the beans, lemon juice and zest, and Amaretto, if using.

Beat the egg whites until stiff and fold into the batter. Pour into a greased 8-inch cake pan. Bake for 1 hour.

Leave in the cake pan until completely cold before turning out. Dust with ground almonds for serving.

Health note We now know that there's more to beans than cheap, filling, and protein-rich benefits. In recent years, the discovery of phytoestrogens has explained why they're so beneficial and protective for women. This is a real PMS, menopause, and anti-osteoporosis cake.

Pumpkin and ginger tart

Serves 6-8

3/4 cup raw sugar (if unavailable,
use light brown)
3 tablespoons ginger syrup (from a
jar of preserved ginger) plus 4-6
pieces of preserved ginger, finely
chopped, to make about
6 tablespoons
2 1/4 pounds pumpkin or
squash flesh, grated
1 (17.3-oz.) package frozen puff
pastry sheet(s), or make
your own

The influences of the Middle East and the Ottoman Empire gave the Sephardi Jews a very sweet tooth. But they also loved all the spices, especially ginger, which combines wonderfully with the already sweet taste of pumpkin. Although this is a very popular Italian Jewish recipe, I have also eaten it in South Africa, where the very mixed Jewish community is extremely fond of pumpkin. They serve it with honey and cinnamon as a vegetable with meat dishes and add a teaspoon of ground cloves to their version of this tart.

This ends up looking like a British treacle tart, but it certainly tastes better and is much more healthy.

Method Preheat the oven to 375°F. Put the sugar, ginger syrup, and pumpkin or squash into a pot and cook over low heat, adding a little water if necessary, until you have a thick paste—about 20 minutes. Stir in the chopped ginger, heat gently for 1 minute and let cool completely.

Use the pastry dough to line a greased baking pan, ideally one that is about 11 x 18 inches. Pour in the ginger and pumpkin mixture and bake for 25 minutes. Serve cold.

Health note In spite of the sugar, this tart is rich in betacarotenes from the pumpkin, and also provides a boost to your circulation thanks to the ginger. Chilblains or varicose veins are wonderful "excuses" for indulging in this tart.

Date tea bread

Serves 6-8

5 lime-blossom tea bags

9 ounces (about 1 3/4–2 cups) whole-wheat flour

2 1/2 teaspoons baking powder

3/4 teaspoon salt

1 egg, beaten

1 cup soft brown sugar

1 pound (about 3–3 1/2 cups) pitted dates, chopped

Dates are one of the great survival foods that have sustained wandering travelers and nomads in the deserts of the Middle East, and camel trains that criss-crossed the silk routes of the ancient world. They grew in vast stretches of land throughout north Africa, Arabia, and Persia. Popular cooked with meat dishes in the Middle East and Elizabethan England, they are used here to make a delicious and healthy tea bread.

There are many variations to this bread. In fact, you can use any combination of any tea and any dried fruit: for example, Earl Grey with mixed exotic fruit, peppermint with dried apples, Lapsang Souchong with prunes.

Method Soak the tea bags in 1 1/4 cups boiling water. Leave until cold, squeeze the tea bags, and discard. Mix the tea with all the other ingredients and let them rest, covered (but not in the fridge), for at least 6 hours.

Preheat the oven to 350°F. Butter a 9 x 5 x 2 1/2-inch bread pan neatly with parchment paper. Pour in the mixture and bake for 30 minutes. Serve when cool.

Health note Rich in energy and fiber and with large amounts of potassium, which is important for the heart and all muscle activity, dates also provide valuable iron, copper, and magnesium. Using lime blossom makes this recipe calming and relaxing: perfect as an evening treat to help you sleep.

Carrot cake with coconut

Serves 6-8

2 tablespoons honey

2/3 cup raw sugar (if unavailable, use light brown)

Scant cup olive oil

3 eggs, beaten

1 teaspoon ground cinnamon

1/4 cup whole-wheat flour

1 3/4 teaspoons baking powder

1/2 teaspoon salt

9 ounces carrots, grated (about 1 3/4–2 cups)

4 ounces (about 1 2/3 cups) dry unsweetened coconut, plus 2 tablespoons for decorating (or decorate with coconut flakes if you prefer)

3/4 cup mixed unsalted nuts, crushed

The Jewish love affair with carrots is obvious when you see how many recipes using this vegetable appear in most Jewish cookbooks. The first time I ate carrot cake was in a tiny village overlooking Lake Zurich in Switzerland, where I'd gone to visit a friend's cousin. I always assumed that this delicious cake was Swiss rather than Jewish until I discovered a variety of *kugels* (cakes, sometimes called puddings) made from vegetables cooked in cake or loaf pans, which were either sweet or savory. Traditional to European Ashkenazim and originally made mostly of potatoes, they're now made from many different and much healthier vegetables, including sweet potatoes.

This is a moist and succulent carrot cake full of health-giving and nutritious ingredients which can be eaten with meat or milk meals.

Method Preheat the oven to 350°F.

Put the honey, sugar, and oil into a bowl and whisk briskly until well combined. Add the eggs and cinnamon and whisk well again. Gradually sift in the flour and whisk until well combined, then stir in the husks that have collected in the sifter. Stir in the carrots, coconut, and nuts. Pour into a greased 7-inch cake pan (if you have one that small) and cook for about 90 minutes.

Let cool and serve sprinkled with the extra coconut.

Three-fruit almond cake

Serves 8

1 orange

1 thin-skinned pink grapefruit

1 lime

³/₄ cup lemon juice

³/₄ cup soft brown sugar

7 ounces (about 2–2 ¹/₄ cups)
* ground almonds*

¹/₂ teaspoon baking powder

5 eggs

Is this a cake or a pudding? Who knows? Who cares? It tastes fantastic and is extremely healthy. You'd be forgiven for imagining that it's a modern Israeli recipe; in fact, it comes from the Jewish community in Stellenbosch, South Africa, a country famous for its wonderful citrus fruits.

Method Put the orange, grapefruit, and lime into a large saucepan, cover with water, and simmer for 90 minutes. Let cool.

Preheat the oven to 400°F.

Cut the fruit in half and remove the seeds. Put the fruit pieces into a blender or food processor along with the lemon juice, sugar, ground almonds, baking powder, and eggs, and whizz until smooth.

Put the mixture into a greased 9-inch cake pan and bake for 40-50 minutes.

Health note Much of the vitamin C will be lost during cooking, but there are protective bioflavonoids in the fruit pith, antibacterial essential oils in the skins, and carotenoids in the pink grapefruit. Protein, minerals, and vitamin E from the almonds, and iron and more protein from the eggs make this an extremely healthy dessert.

Honey cake (lekach)

Serves 6-8

1/2 cup honey

2 eggs

1/2 cup raw sugar (if unavailable, use light brown)

3 tablespoons olive oil

2/3 cup coffee

1 1/4 cups white flour

1 1/4 cups whole-wheat flour

3 3/4 teaspoons baking powder

1 3/4 teaspoons salt

1/2 teaspoon ground cloves

1 teaspoon ground ginger

3 tablespoons slivered almonds, for sprinkling

There are almost as many recipes for honey cake (lekach) as there are Jewish cooks. Although they're all similar, communities and even individuals add their own touches to the basic recipe. Traditionally served during Rosh Hashanah, the Jewish New Year, it is eaten as a reflection of our prayers for a sweet year to come. In our house, it was something of a mixed blessing; this recipe was given to my mother by her Dutch mother-in-law, and at every New Year celebration it was a reminder of my father's parents, grandparents, his great-grandmother, brothers, sister, uncles, aunts, nieces, and nephews who vanished into the Holocaust of the Second World War. Only his youngest brother and his wife (Jo and Henny) survived, thanks to the incredible bravery of a Catholic family who hid them in the cellars under their farmhouse.

Method Preheat the oven to 375°F.

Warm the honey in a small pan. Beat the eggs and sugar together.

Add the oil, warmed honey, and coffee to the egg mixture. Sift in the remaining dry ingredients (except the almonds), add 2/3 cup warm water, and beat well. Turn the mixture into a greased 9-inch loaf pan and sprinkle with the slivered almonds. Bake for 1 hour.

Health note As cakes go (and this one always does) this is pretty healthy, but not when eaten in the Dutch manner: spread thickly with butter or with a slice of the wonderful Leiden cheese, made with spicy caraway seeds.

Prune cheesecake

Serves 4-6

1 frozen pie crust, or make
* your own*
1/3 cup (3/4 stick) unsalted butter
1/4 cup superfine sugar
3 small eggs, beaten
14 ounces (about 1 3/4 cups) curd
* cheese, drained (if unavailable,*
* use a mixture of cottage cheese,*
* drained, and cream cheese)*
6 large ready-to-eat prunes,
* cut up to the size of raisins*
Grated zest of 1 large lemon

Cooked cheesecake is one of the most popular recipes from German Jewish cooking, and it is one that has spread far beyond the Jewish kitchen and bakery to become universally accepted—nowhere more so than in America, where it's a national dish. I find this type of cheesecake infinitely preferable to the non-cooked versions, which are normally made with processed, cream-like cheeses, then refrigerated to make them solidify.

Many older Jewish women made their own curd cheese by hanging cheese-cloth bags of soured milk, like my mother did, on the washing line. Dairy foods such as this cake are a traditional feature of the festival of Shavuot, the sixth day of the Hebrew month of *Sivan*: May to June in the Western calender. This celebrates both the festival of the First Fruits and the time when the Torah (the Law) was handed down by God to the Jewish people on Mount Sinai.

Method Preheat oven to 450°F.

If making your own dough, roll it out and line a greased tart pan, 7-inch diameter if you have one—otherwise use an 8-inch pan. Prick the bottom several times with a fork. Line the pie shell with non-stick baking paper, cover with dried beans, and bake for 10-15 minutes. Remove the beans and paper and bake for 5 more minutes to crisp the crust.

Cream together the butter and sugar and beat in the eggs and cheese. Stir in the prunes and lemon zest. Put the mixture into the pie shell.

Put into the preheated oven, then immediately turn the heat down to 350°F. Bake until the filling is set and the pastry golden—about 25 minutes.

Health note The addition of prunes instead of the more traditional raisins gives this recipe protective qualities in addition to the protein and calcium from the curd cheese.

Index

Acknowledgements I've wanted to write this book for many years as I am passionate about Jewish food, so first I must thank Kyle Cathie for giving me this opportunity. Working with Muna Reyal has been an absolute joy, thanks to her enormous enthusiasm and creativity. Great thanks are due to Jan Baldwin for her beautiful food photography and to Vanessa Courtier for her imaginative location photos and beautiful design. I'd also like to express my gratitude to the Jewish Museum, London and curator, Jennifer Marin, for the time and trouble they took to make so much material available. Finally, yet another opportunity for Sally and me to work with our favorite and incredibly efficient editor, Jamie Ambrose.

Thanks also to The Brick Lane Beigel Bake, 159 Brick Lane, London E1 6SB; Hampstead Seafoods, 78 Hampstead High Street, London NW3; Hampstead Tea Rooms, 9 South End Road, London NW3 2PT; Panzer's, 13-19 Circus Road, London NW8; Pomona, 179 Haverstock Hill, London NW3 4QS; Sam's Fish and Chips, 68-70 Golders Green Road, London NW11 8LN; Six-13, 19 Wigmore Street, London W1U 1PH; Steimatzky Hasifria, 46 Golders Green Road, London NW11 8LL for allowing us to photograph their premises.